IT'S ABOUT THYME

IT'S ABOUT THYME

FABULOUS FIVE INC
STEPHANIE McKEE · PHYLLIS JONES
DEBBIE RUBIN · JAN TONROY · DIANE EARL

FABULOUS FIVE, INC.

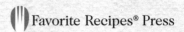 Favorite Recipes® Press

Fabulous Five, Inc., began in 1987 when five Texas women began cooking a monthly dinner together in their homes. From the first meeting, their time together turned into a major cooking, traveling, and sharing extravaganza that inspired their popular cookbook. *It's About Thyme* was published by Fabulous Five, Inc., and is part of the *Snooty Women®* series. This cookbook is a collection of favorite recipes, which are not necessarily original recipes. Fabulous Five, Inc., 1833 Old Annetta Road, Aledo, Texas 76008. www.cookingwiththefabfive.com | 817-441-9781

ISBN: 978-0-9709147-1-2
Library of Congress Catalog Number: 2015950340
Printed in China
10 9 8 7 6 5 4 3 2 1

It's About Thyme For MORE Great Friends, Fabulous Food, and Spirited Fun! was edited, designed, and manufactured by Favorite Recipes Press (FRP) in collaboration with Fabulous Five, Inc. FRP works with top chefs, food and appliance manufacturers, restaurants and resorts, health organizations, Junior Leagues, and nonprofit organizations to create award-winning cookbooks and other food-related products. FRP is an imprint of Southwestern Publishing Group, Inc., 2451 Atrium Way, Nashville, Tennessee 37214. Southwestern Publishing Group is a wholly owned subsidiary of Southwestern/Great American, Inc., Nashville, Tennessee. www.frpbooks.com | 800-358-0560

Christopher G. Capen, President, Southwestern Publishing Group
Sheila Thomas, President and Publisher, Favorite Recipes Press
Vicky Shea, Senior Art Director
Kristin Connelly, Managing Editor
Linda Brock, Editor
Rhonda Brock, Proofreader

Greetings

We are delighted to return with a new cookbook that celebrates our twenty-eight-year friendship as the Fabulous Five, a friendship that is deeply rooted in our shared love of preparing and presenting exciting and delicious meals. The five of us—Diane Earl, Phyllis Jones, Stephanie McKee, Debbie Rubin, and Jan Tonroy— met as young businesswomen in Lubbock, Texas, way back in 1987, and quickly built a fast friendship around our mutual appreciation for adventurous eating. We have always loved to cook together, and what began as a monthly ritual of preparing glamorous dinners at each other's homes soon expanded to include weekend retreats and girlfriend vacations. After Debbie and Jan found professional positions in Fort Worth, it also included elaborate two-city holiday gatherings for our growing families.

In 2001, we published our first cookbook, *Always Enough Thyme For Great Friends, Fabulous Food, and Spirited Fun!* The book was a resounding success, and people have continued to ask us when we will publish another. Finally, after fifteen years, we have coordinated our ever-expanding collection of Fab Five–tested recipes, and for obvious reasons, we have titled our second cookbook *It's About Thyme For MORE Great Friends, Fabulous Food, and Spirited Fun!*

During these fifteen years, our friendship has stayed strong and always a little bit crazy, as we've met the inevitable challenges of our personal and professional lives, sharing the joys with fun and laughter and the sadness with sympathy and tears. Diane has kept us all close while building a stellar career with United Supermarkets; she is now serving as Senior Director of Prepared Foods. Debbie is also a professional culinarian and continues with her longtime position as Manager of Catering at the City Club in Fort Worth. She has been free of breast cancer for fifteen years now, and we celebrate her resilience every day. Stephanie has come through the heart-wrenching challenges of losing her husband to illness and now continues with her career at GVH Distribution. In 2010, Phyllis decided on the single life and is now Director of Development for Ronald McDonald House in Lubbock, relishing the many opportunities she has to engage with the world as an independent agent. Jan is blissfully anticipating her retirement as a very successful teacher of business in the Aledo Independent School System.

Throughout these years, we have deepened our relationships by respecting our demanding schedules, and our cooking habits have changed with the times. Today, we gather to cook in a more casual manner than in the early years, when we were constantly coordinating mealtime extravaganzas. Our seven children—six boys and one girl—were raised together, attending Fab Five gatherings during the holidays and summertime. The youngest is now at the University of Texas-Arlington, and the rest have gone on to their professional lives. We are gratified they have remained good friends and built their own distinctive relationships with each other. Two of the Fab Five children have married, and we look forward to celebrating as the Fab Five at all the weddings to come.

Today, we spend more time with each other on the road than in our homes, gleefully orchestrating periodic destination get-togethers. Our ever-evolving friendship seems to thrive in fresh environments, where we share the dining experience, a love of music and dancing, and our ready collection of enticing recipes. *It's About Thyme* presents our favorite combinations for lazy morning brunches, hearty lunches, the cocktail hour, and evening meals ending with delicious desserts. We are pleased to share our discoveries and hope they will help nurture the kind of camaraderie a wonderful meal is always meant to bring.

The Fabulous Five
2001

Acknowledgments

We would like to thank all of our dear friends—some longtime, some new—for their steadfast encouragement, their good company, and their generous contributions of favorite recipes to our book.

The Fabulous Five
2016

Dedication

We dedicate this book to our families for their love, support, and companionship through all these years. Please know that we consider ourselves the luckiest of women for having you as a vital part of our lives.

The Fab Five Children
2010

Contents

Destination Celebrations

O ne day, we woke up and realized that in very short order, we were all going to turn fifty years old! Naturally, it came as a shock, but we soon recovered when we realized this epic milestone was the perfect opportunity for five fabulous destination celebrations, organized around each birthday and treated as a surprise party for the lucky fifty-year-old recipient.

Spa Time for Jan's Fiftieth: Jan was the first of us to reach the Big Five-O, and we arrived at her Fort Worth home in a limousine, sporting spectacular hats as a tribute to the significance of the occasion. Of course, our first stop was a grocery store. Parading through as the Big Hat Mutual Admiration Society, we loaded up on wine, cheese, and the other necessities to prepare our favorite munchies for a long slumber-party weekend. Supplies in tow, we headed for Dallas, frequented a few hot spots to get the party rolling, and then settled into the relaxing atmosphere of a lovely Dallas resort, where we indulged ourselves with massages, facials, gal-pal time in the sauna, and a spectacular happy birthday dinner for the guest of honor. Of course, the weekend was full of laughter and constant conversation as we celebrated Jan as our trailblazer into the age of wisdom.

Cruising with Stephanie at Fifty: When Stephanie turned fifty, Jan took it upon herself to organize the big celebration, and big it was. We all headed for Galveston, Texas, where we surprised Stephanie with a four-day trip on the Carnival Cruise Line sailing the Caribbean. We quickly realized this leisurely aquatic environment suited many of the natural habits of the Fab Five. We were thrilled with the vast selection of food we savored and shared in excess through breakfast, lunch, and dinner. We danced the nights away in the jubilant club atmosphere of the ship and enjoyed a fun-filled day in Cozumel, snorkeling, boating, shopping, and relishing the island scenery. We also got in some gambling. When Diane won big at blackjack, she very generously shared her winnings with the rest of us, and we quickly spent it all with joyous abandon. Of course, Stephanie was treated to a fancy birthday dinner aboard ship with a big cake to hold all those candles and a rousing chorus of "Happy Birthday" from staff, girlfriends, and fellow passengers. As it happened, Stephanie was the only one awake when the bill arrived. At first, she thought it was a phone book and had some difficulty processing the extravagance of her birthday event. We, however, thought she was worth every penny and loved the excuse to take another memorable excursion, enjoying each other's company as the Fabulous Five.

Debbie's Rocky Mountain High Fiftieth: For Debbie's fiftieth, Stephanie planned a spectacular All-American road trip to Colorado. We gathered in Lubbock, rented an SUV, and headed west, listening to our 70s favorites and singing at the top of our lungs in memory of those joyous and outrageous times when we were just beginning life's adventure. We withstood Debbie's constant probing and kept the destination a surprise until we arrived in Denver for our first night's stay in the charming and very classy Hotel Monaco. After a leisurely dinner, we turned in early to be rested for our next day's journey high up in the mountains, where we stayed for the rest of the trip at a gorgeous home in Vail, Colorado. The house was perfectly appointed for our late-morning, long-conversation brunches and the preparation of some of the recipes we had all been collecting. As an acknowledgment of her advancing age, Debbie had begun to compile her bucket list, and the famous Red Rock Amphitheater was definitely a top contender. Stephanie knew this—Stephanie always knows everything—so she booked tickets and off we went to this fabulous, acoustically pristine, natural open-air theater, surrounded by the majesty of the great Rocky Mountains. We boogied down all night to the live performances of John Mellencamp and John Fogerty, once again singing at the top of our lungs to the music of our youth, confident that Fogerty and Mellencamp's classic rock creations would be around for us to enjoy until we reached another fifty. The finale to this "Rocky Mountain High" was a grand birthday dinner at Sweet Basil in Vail, formally celebrating this significant passage in the life of our BFF, Debbie Rubin.

A Houseboat Haven for Diane's Fiftieth: When Diane's fiftieth rolled around, she was exhausted from the challenges of her very exciting job and requested an uncomplicated gathering for the rare chance to unwind. Debbie picked the perfect place. We all met up in Dallas and took off in a rented van for another liberating road trip to an out-of-Texas destination. We always tease Diane about doing the head bobble to music that speaks to her. Toe tapping and nodding her head up and down are the extent of her "getting down with the music," so Debbie presented Diane with a Bobblehead doll dressed in a bikini to adorn the dash of the van. And the Diane replica just bobbled away as we listened and sang to liberatingly loud music on the long ride to Arkansas, taking the back roads to Lake Ouachita, our destination near Little Rock. On arrival at the lake, we were officially ferried to an island in the middle of the waters, where we stayed on a 1950s houseboat in glorious isolation for the coming days. Always eager to add performance to any occasion, Debbie inspired us with a take on *Gilligan's Island*. Diane played The Skipper, Stephanie played Mary Ann, Phyllis played Ginger, and Jan played The Professor. Then, we proceeded to do exactly what we love to do most. Meeting the challenge of our Spartan conditions, we cooked great late breakfasts and elaborate dinners, drank lots of wine, and caught up on our lives, laughing and enjoying each other's company until the boatman returned. We did manage to spend one day in civilized surroundings, exploring Hot Springs, but mostly this was a fiftieth birthday party marked by the slow time of the lakeside and the comfortable companionship of old, dear friends, sharing many laughs at our own expense and at life's passages.

New York, New York for Phyllis' Fiftieth: To complete the magic circle of fiftieth birthday celebrations, Diane planned a spectacular surprise party for Phyllis: a grand trip to New York City, Phyllis' favorite place on the planet, as we all knew. Of course, Diane worked very hard to fill our days with the kinds of events only New York has to offer. We took in *Jersey Boys* on Broadway and pooled our resources for Phyllis to have a shopping trip to Tiffany's. We consider city barhopping an art form, and barhop we did, all over Manhattan. Probably the most unusual club we visited was Please Don't Tell, where people enter through a hot dog restaurant by sliding into a classic phone booth and then speaking to a hostess, for the phone-booth doors to magically open into an upscale New York hotspot. We also frequented a very interesting Russian bar that served only Russian vodka. It's a good thing the Fab Five know their vodka, because no English was spoken there. Our charming hotel did not have a bar, but we quickly found a quaint establishment right next door and struck up an acquaintance with two English couples on their first trip to the United States. At our nightly sessions, we made sure to enlighten them and entertain them with a heavy dose of Texas in the midst of their Big Apple experience. To catch our breaths, we decided to see the movie *Sex and the City* on opening weekend. What a treat for us to see this movie all about a feisty group of steadfast girlfriends that ends with one of them, Samantha, celebrating her fiftieth birthday! Coincidence? We think not.

The Fab Five Sixtieth in Tuscany: Through our round of fiftieth birthday extravaganzas, we discovered many new ways to enjoy each other's company and determined that, from now on, we would definitely mark each milestone birthday with destination celebrations. For our sixtieth, we decided to commemorate this epic event all at once with an eight-day trip to Tuscany, a place that has always evoked for us the kind of casual elegance in food and friendship we value so much.

None of us had ever been to Italy, so we planned meticulously for our adventure across the sea and contracted with a tour company to help us navigate this *terra incognita*. We arrived in Rome and found we had a four-hour wait for the rest of the tour group to arrive, so we practiced the grand art of patience by finding a wine shop, buying a couple of bottles, and settling in to enjoy our own good company by the Tyrrhenian Sea. Finally, we were off to Montecatini and the

Hotel Adua, our home base for the tour.

Each day, we rode the bus to another site to experience the soft, timeless pleasures of the region. Our tour guide for the whole trip was a delightful young man named Christian, who spoke mighty fine English with a lilting Italian accent and shared the richness of the culture with us at every turn. From the glamorous cities of Florence and Siena to the ancient fishing villages of Cinque Terre to the charming rural hamlets of San Gimignano and Greve to the winery at Castello Vicchiomaggio, we were immersed in the dynamic culture of the region for seven glorious days.

We ate our first gnocchi in Florence, and those light little dumplings became a point of comparison and contrast for the rest of the trip. Dining at Marina Piccola Ristorante in Manarola, with the backdrop of lopsided cliff houses perched high above a roiling sea, we shared plates of fish, pesto, limoncello, local wine, and gelato with great enthusiasm and celebrated the fresh and forthright tastes of Italy with a growing appreciation. In Siena, we ate at the La Costa Bar, right on the Piazza del Campo, happy to watch the people touring the square and to revel in the beauty of the city and its time-honored traditions, including Tuscan pastries at the famous Pasticcerie Nannini.

Our tour of the wine country took us deep into the heart of the evocative Tuscan landscape that figures so prominently in the backgrounds of Renaissance paintings. The trip included a visit to Greve and the first butcher shop in Italy, where we sampled highly flavored salami and cheese and stocked up for snacks. At Castello Vicchiomaggio, we were treated to a wine tasting, followed by a delicious meal in the stately dining room. We discovered that Leonardo da Vinci painted the *Mona Lisa* during a stay at this castle and were delighted to visit his hometown of Vinci on our return trip to Montecatini, with the chance to sample and buy olives of virtually every taste and hue from the surrounding nearby orchards.

Our last day in Tuscany was a lazy, free day, and we happily settled into our tried-and-true habit of sleeping late and indulging in a serious and satisfying brunch in Montecatini Alto, the old village at the top of the hill where we stayed. The view of the city was inspiring, and we enjoyed the slow time to share our feelings and perceptions of this glorious trip back in time. Did we mention shopping? Well, we did at every turn: gold and leather in Florence, marble souvenirs in Carrera, and window-shopping in all the charming villages. We managed one last round in Montecatini Alto before returning to our neighborhood for a pizza dinner.

Back in Rome for our last night before the flight home, we stayed at La Griffe, a lovely hotel in the very heart of ancient Rome, where we took full advantage of the location to stroll the narrow streets and immerse ourselves in the ages. As we drifted and chatted, we noticed a young man beckoning us to come eat at this very inconspicuous restaurant, so we did, and we all agree this was the most memorable dining experience of the whole trip. He seated us on the third-floor rooftop of his family restaurant. He was the waiter and his mother the cook. The meal began with a homemade soup and delicious dishes just kept coming. Our habit of passing our plates around to share our selections with each other was rather unnerving to the young man, but he took it in stride, probably because we were the very first of the evening to enter the restaurant. We noticed throughout our trip that we always arrived a bit early and ate a bit fast for the Italian rhythm of dining, and this meal at the tiny restaurant Oratorio was no exception.

After a coffee on the rooftop, with a bird's eye view of ancient Rome at twilight, we joined our group for a tour of the famous touchstones of the city, ending at the Square of All-Night Partying, where we joined in the revelry before returning to our hotel for a very short night of sleep.

Everything on our trip was a feast for the eyes and all of the other senses, and we are already planning our next Fab Five destination celebration to the Mediterranean. Milestones, we have determined, are relative and need not have anything to do with birthdays or aging. We love to travel together, share food discoveries, and keep each other company. That's more than enough to engage in a whole series of destination celebrations.

Fiftieth Birthday Trips

Fiftieth Birthday Trips

Italy Trip 2013

Buffalo Gap, Texas

BRUNCH
OVER EASY

Brunch is always our favorite meal. We like to wake up slowly and ease into the day with a delicious combination of sweet breads, eggs every which way, fruit, and exotic additions that lend themselves to hours of coffee and conversation. We are always adding to our brunch recipe collection and hope these new discoveries inspire a host of late-morning gatherings that spread good cheer and provide a tasty selection of gratifying brunchables.

Debbie's Chicken Chilaquiles

This is a wonderful brunch dish. Just add fresh fruit and scrambled eggs, and you're done!

2 cups shredded rotisserie chicken

½ cup chopped green onions

½ cup (2 ounces) shredded Monterey Jack cheese with jalapeños, divided

2 tablespoons grated Parmesan cheese

1 teaspoon chili powder

¼ teaspoon salt

¼ teaspoon black pepper

1 (11-ounce) can tomatillos, drained

¼ cup chopped fresh cilantro

1 (4-ounce) can chopped green chilies, drained

¾ cup low-fat milk

12 corn tortillas

Nonstick cooking spray

Preheat the oven to 375 degrees.

Combine the chicken, green onions, ¼ cup Monterey Jack cheese, Parmesan cheese, chili powder, salt and pepper in a medium bowl and mix well. Place the tomatillos, cilantro, chilies and milk in a food processor or blender; process until smooth.

Heat the tortillas according to the package directions. Pour ⅓ cup of the tomatillo mixture over the bottom of a 9 x11-inch baking dish coated with nonstick cooking spray. Arrange 4 tortillas in the dish. Spread with half the chicken mixture. Repeat the layers using the remaining tortillas and chicken mixture, ending with the tortillas.

Pour the remaining tomatillo mixture over the tortillas and sprinkle with the remaining Monterey Jack cheese. Bake for 20 minutes or until hot and bubbly.

I get by with A Little Help From My Friends.
JOHN LENNON

Glazed Hot Ham and Cheese Sandwiches

These small glazed and baked sandwiches are great for a meal, picnic, formal affair or brunch. Easy to make, always delicious and everyone loves them. These also freeze well.

2 packages Hawaiian rolls

1½ pounds sliced ham

1 pound sliced Swiss cheese

½ cup butter

¼ cup sugar

¼ cup honey mustard

2 teaspoons poppy seeds

1½ teaspoons Worcestershire sauce

1 tablespoon onion flakes (optional)

Preheat the oven to 350 degrees.

Cut off the tops of the rolls without separating them into individual rolls.

Line a 9x13-inch pan with the bottom layer of the rolls. Layer with the ham and cheese. Replace the tops of the rolls.

Mix the butter, sugar, honey mustard, poppy seeds, Worcestershire sauce and onion flakes in a saucepan. Bring to a boil; boil for 2 minutes. Pour the sauce evenly over the sandwiches. Place the pan of rolls on a baking sheet to prevent burning. Bake, covered, for 20 minutes. Remove the cover and bake for 10 to 15 minutes.

All happiness depends on a leisurely breakfast.

JOHN GUNTHER

Green Chile, Bacon and Cheese Egg Bake

Nonstick cooking spray

12 ounces grated sharp Cheddar cheese

2 (4-ounce) cans diced green chilies, drained

4 large eggs

3 cups milk

1 cup all-purpose flour

½ teaspoon salt

8 slices of bacon, cooked and crumbled

Preheat the oven to 350 degrees. Spray a 9x13-inch baking dish with nonstick cooking spray.

Mix the cheese and chilies in a bowl. Spread over the bottom of the prepared dish.

Whisk the eggs, milk, flour and salt in a medium bowl. Pour over the cheese mixture. Sprinkle with the bacon. Bake for 40 to 45 minutes or until the mixture is bubbly, the eggs are thoroughly cooked and a wooden pick inserted into the center comes out clean.

NOTE: The recipe may be halved and baked in an 8x8-inch baking dish.

First we eat, then we do everything else.
MFK Fisher

Eggs Taos

We made these while staying in a wonderful house in Santa Fe on our Fall Retreat.

1 large garlic clove, minced

½ onion, chopped

4 tablespoons butter

¼ cup all-purpose flour

2 cups milk

1 (7-ounce) can chopped green chilies

½ teaspoon salt

¼ teaspoon freshly ground black pepper

10 eggs, lightly beaten

2 avocados, seeded, peeled and mashed

8 flour tortillas

3 cups shredded Cheddar and/or Monterey Jack cheese

1 cup sour cream

2 tomatoes, chopped

Preheat the oven to 350 degrees.

Sauté the garlic and onion in the butter in a large skillet over high heat. Stir in the flour. Add the milk and cook until the sauce is thickened, whisking constantly. Add the chilies, salt and pepper. Remove from the heat and set aside.

Cook the eggs in a large skillet, stirring to scramble; set aside. Spoon 2 tablespoons of the sauce, ⅛ of the eggs and ⅛ of the avocado onto each tortilla. Roll to enclose the filling and arrange seam side down in a 9x13-inch baking dish. Spoon the remaining sauce over the tortillas. Sprinkle with the cheese. Bake for 15 to 20 minutes or until heated through. Top with the sour cream and tomatoes.

Breakfast Casserole with Asparagus, Prosciutto and Cheese

Perfect for brunch or morning bridal or baby showers. A very pretty dish.

Salt to taste

1 bunch of asparagus

1 tablespoon extra-virgin olive oil

1½ cups finely chopped onions

1¼ cups finely chopped prosciutto

3 cups shredded Cheddar cheese

8 cups cubed crusty bread, such as French or Italian (1-inch cubes)

Nonstick cooking spray

8 large eggs, lightly beaten

3 cups half-and-half

2 tablespoons minced fresh chives or scallions including green tops

1¼ teaspoons salt

1¼ teaspoons sweet paprika

¼ teaspoon cayenne pepper

¾ cup grated Parmesan cheese

Fill a large pot three-fourths full of water and add enough salt to season. Bring to a boil over high heat. Prepare a large bowl full of ice water to use as an ice bath.

Break the tough ends off the asparagus. Add the asparagus to the pot of boiling water and cook for 1 minute or just until tender and bright green. Transfer the asparagus to the ice bath using a skimmer to stop the cooking process. Let stand until the asparagus is chilled; drain well. Pat dry using paper towels and set aside.

Heat the olive oil in a small sauté pan over medium-high heat. Add the onions and 1 or 2 pinches of salt. Cook for 4 minutes or until the onions are tender, stirring occasionally. Remove from the heat and set aside to cool.

Combine the asparagus, onions, prosciutto, Cheddar cheese and bread in a large bowl. Toss gently to mix. Transfer to a 9x13-inch baking dish sprayed with nonstick cooking spray, spreading the mixture in an even layer.

Whisk the eggs, half-and-half, chives, 1¼ teaspoons salt, paprika and cayenne pepper in a bowl until thoroughly mixed. Pour over the asparagus mixture. Cover with plastic wrap and store in the refrigerator for 4 hours to overnight. Remove the casserole from the refrigerator about 30 minutes before baking to allow it to reach room temperature.

Preheat the oven to 375 degrees. Remove the plastic wrap from the baking dish and cover the dish with aluminum foil. Bake for 45 minutes.

Remove the foil and sprinkle the Parmesan cheese evenly over the top. Bake, uncovered, for 15 minutes or until the top is golden brown and puffed and the casserole is cooked through when tested with a knife.

Transfer the baking dish to a wire rack and let stand to cool for 10 to 15 minutes. Cut into squares to serve.

Winter Fruit Compote

½ cup sugar

⅓ cup water

½ vanilla bean, split lengthwise

1½ teaspoons fresh lime or lemon juice

1 tablespoon butter

1 Golden Delicious or other sweet, firm apple, peeled, cored and cut into ½-inch cubes

1 kiwi, cut into ¼-inch slices

¼ cup dried cranberries

½ cup cubed fresh pineapple

¼ cup chopped pecans (optional; Diane recommends!)

Combine the sugar and water in a small heavy saucepan. Scrape the vanilla bean seeds into the saucepan and add the vanilla bean shell. Cook over low heat until the sugar is dissolved, stirring constantly. Boil over high heat for 1 minute. Cool the syrup completely.

Transfer the syrup to a bowl and discard the vanilla bean shell. Stir in the lime juice. Cover and chill for 1 to 12 hours.

Melt the butter in a skillet over medium heat. Add the apple and sauté for 2 minutes or until the apple is slightly tender. Add the apple, kiwi, dried cranberries and pineapple to the syrup and stir gently to coat all the fruit. Stir in the pecans.

Breakfast Enchiladas

This can be made the day before, and then baked and served the day of your event. So good!

CHEESE SAUCE

- 5 tablespoons butter
- ⅓ cup all-purpose flour
- 3 cups milk
- 2 cups (8 ounces) shredded Cheddar cheese
- 1 (4-ounce) can chopped green chilies, undrained
- ¾ teaspoon salt

ENCHILADAS

- 1 pound ground hot pork sausage
- 2 tablespoons butter
- 4 green onions, thinly sliced
- 2 tablespoons chopped fresh cilantro
- 14 large eggs, beaten
- ¾ teaspoon salt
- ½ teaspoon pepper
- 8 (8-inch) flour tortillas
- 1 cup (4 ounces) shredded Pepper Jack cheese
- Grape tomato halves, sliced green onions and chopped fresh cilantro for garnish

For the Cheese Sauce, melt the butter in a heavy saucepan over medium-low heat. Add the flour and whisk until smooth. Cook for 1 minute, whisking constantly. Add the milk gradually, whisking constantly. Cook over medium heat for 5 minutes or until thickened, whisking constantly. Remove from the heat and whisk in the cheese, chilies and salt.

For the Enchiladas, preheat the oven to 350 degrees. Grease a 9x13-inch baking dish lightly.

Brown the sausage in a large nonstick skillet over medium-high heat, stirring to crumble. Remove the sausage from the pan and drain well by pressing between paper towels.

Melt the butter in a large nonstick skillet over medium heat. Add the green onions and cilantro. Sauté for 1 minute. Add the eggs, salt and pepper. Cook, without stirring, until the eggs begin to set on the bottom. Draw a spatula across the bottom of the pan to form large curds. Cook until the eggs are thickened but still moist. Do not stir constantly. Remove from the heat. Fold in 1½ cups of the Cheese Sauce and the sausage.

Spoon about ⅓ cup of the egg mixture down the center of each tortilla and roll to enclose the filling. Arrange seam side down in the prepared baking dish. Pour the remaining Cheese Sauce evenly over the tortillas and sprinkle evenly with the Pepper Jack cheese.

Bake for 30 minutes or until the sauce is hot and bubbly. Garnish with grape tomato halves, green onions and cilantro.

Baked Cheese Grits Casserole

4 tablespoons butter, melted

1 pound ground pork sausage

1 tablespoon finely diced onion

1 cup milk

6 eggs, beaten

1 cup grits (cooked in 4 cups water)

1 (6-ounce) package corn muffin mix

1 teaspoon SPIKE® Original Magic seasoning (can be found in health food stores), or any other seasoning you like

8 ounces Colby or Monterey Jack cheese, shredded

½ teaspoon paprika

Preheat the oven to 350 degrees. Pour the melted butter evenly over the bottom of a 9x12-inch baking pan.

Brown the sausage with the onion in a skillet, stirring to crumble the sausage; drain. Combine the milk and eggs in a large bowl and mix well. Stir in the grits, corn muffin mix and seasoning. Spread the sausage mixture over the bottom of the prepared baking pan. Spread with the grits mixture and sprinkle with the cheese. Sprinkle with paprika. Bake for 1 hour or until the casserole is firm in the middle. Let stand for 5 minutes before serving.

Spanish Potato Omelet

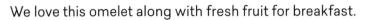

We love this omelet along with fresh fruit for breakfast.

½ cup extra-virgin olive oil, divided

1 pound red or white potatoes, peeled and cut into ⅛-inch-thick slices

Salt and freshly ground black pepper to taste

1 large onion, sliced

1 red bell pepper, stemmed, seeded and sliced

1 garlic clove, minced

6 eggs

½ cup minced fresh parsley

Preheat the oven to 375 degrees.

Heat about half of the olive oil in a large nonstick ovenproof skillet over medium heat. Add the potatoes and season liberally with salt and pepper. Cook for 20 minutes or until the potatoes are tender, turning gently occasionally. Remove using a slotted spoon. Add the remaining olive oil to the pan. Cook the onion and bell pepper in the olive oil for 10 minutes or until tender, stirring occasionally. Add the garlic and cook for 2 minutes. Return the potatoes to the skillet and reduce the heat to medium-low. Cook for 5 minutes, turning the mixture with a spatula occasionally. Reduce the heat to low.

Beat the eggs with the parsley in a bowl. Pour the egg mixture over the potato mixture. Shake the pan to distribute the eggs evenly and cook for 5 minutes without stirring. Transfer the skillet to the oven and bake for 10 minutes or until the mixture is set. Let stand to cool to room temperature before cutting into chunks or wedges.

Vegetable Pasta Oven Omelet

Great vegetarian option.

3 sun-dried tomatoes in oil

1 small onion, chopped

½ red bell pepper, diced

3 garlic cloves, minced

2 tablespoons extra-virgin olive oil

1 small zucchini, diced

3 ounces cream cheese, softened

7 ounces vermicelli, cooked according to the package directions

6 large eggs

¾ cup shredded Parmesan cheese, divided

¾ cup milk

1 teaspoon dried Italian seasoning

½ teaspoon salt

¼ teaspoon pepper

Preheat the oven to 375 degrees.

Drain the sun-dried tomatoes well, pressing them between layers of paper towels. Chop the tomatoes. Sauté the onion, bell pepper and garlic in the olive oil in a 12-inch nonstick ovenproof skillet for 5 minutes or until tender. Add the sun-dried tomatoes and zucchini and sauté for 3 minutes. Add the cream cheese and cook until melted, stirring constantly. Add the pasta and toss to coat.

Whisk the eggs, ½ cup of the Parmesan cheese, milk, Italian seasoning, salt and pepper in a bowl until well mixed. Pour over the pasta mixture in the skillet. Bake for 25 to 30 minutes or until set. Sprinkle with the remaining Parmesan cheese. Let stand for 10 minutes before serving.

Spinach, Mushroom and Feta Crustless Quiche

Nonstick cooking spray

1 (10-ounce) box frozen spinach, thawed

8 ounces fresh mushrooms

½ teaspoon minced garlic

Salt and pepper to taste

2 ounces feta cheese, crumbled

4 large eggs

1 cup milk

¼ cup grated Parmesan cheese

½ cup shredded mozzarella cheese

Preheat the oven to 350 degrees. Spray a pie plate with nonstick cooking spray.

Drain the spinach in a colander. Rinse the mushrooms and slice them thinly. Sauté the mushrooms and garlic in a skillet coated with nonstick cooking spray over medium-high heat for 5 to 7 minutes or until the mushrooms release all of their moisture and no more water remains on the bottom of the skillet. Sprinkle with salt and pepper.

Squeeze the spinach to remove any excess moisture. Spread the spinach over the bottom of the prepared pie plate. Add the mushroom mixture and feta cheese.

Whisk the eggs in a medium bowl until smooth. Add the milk and Parmesan cheese and whisk to mix. Pour over the layers.

Sprinkle with the mozzarella cheese. Place the pie plate on a baking sheet for easy transfer into the oven. Bake for 45 to 60 minutes or until the quiche is golden brown and the center is set. Slice and serve.

Chile Relleno Torta

8 ounces Cheddar cheese, grated

8 ounces Monterey Jack cheese, grated

5 eggs

½ teaspoon salt

⅓ cup all-purpose flour

1⅔ cups half-and-half

1 (4-ounce) can diced green chilies, drained

¼ cup picante sauce

Preheat the oven to 375 degrees. Butter a 10-inch pie plate.

Mix the Cheddar cheese and Monterey Jack cheese and spread evenly in the prepared pie plate. Beat the eggs and salt in a mixing bowl; add the flour gradually, beating constantly. Beat in the half-and-half. Strain the mixture if lumpy.

Pour over the cheese in the pie plate. Spoon the chilies carefully onto the egg mixture. Top with the picante sauce. Bake for 45 minutes or until the center is set.

Ham and Blue Cheese Frittata

8 eggs

1 cup milk

12 cherry tomatoes, cut into halves

⅓ cup frozen peas

2 scallions, thinly sliced

1½ cups diced thick-cut ham

2 ounces blue cheese, crumbled

¼ teaspoon kosher salt

⅛ teaspoon freshly ground black pepper

Preheat the oven to 400 degrees. Grease a 9-inch square baking dish lightly.

Whisk the eggs and milk in a bowl. Add the tomatoes, peas, scallions, ham, blue cheese, salt and pepper and mix well. Pour into the prepared baking dish and bake for 40 minutes or until the frittata is puffed and golden brown and the center is set.

Fab Five Frittatas in Mason Jars

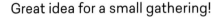

Great idea for a small gathering!

8 ounces ground turkey breakfast sausage

½ pound fingerling potatoes, cut into small cubes

8 ounces fresh spinach, stemmed and coarsely chopped

Kosher salt and freshly cracked black pepper to taste

8 large eggs

1 teaspoon cayenne pepper

¼ cup milk

1 cup shredded sharp Cheddar cheese

Nonstick cooking spray

Brown the sausage in a large skillet, stirring to crumble. Stir in the potatoes and spinach and cook until the spinach is wilted, stirring frequently. Season with salt and pepper. Remove from the heat.

Beat the eggs lightly in a medium bowl. Season with salt, pepper and cayenne pepper. Whisk in the milk and cheese. Set aside.

Preheat the oven to 375 degrees. Spray six 8-ounce glass canning jars very liberally with nonstick cooking spray (do not put the lids on).

Divide the sausage mixture evenly among the jars. Top off each jar with the egg mixture, leaving 1 inch of headspace. Place the jars in a baking dish filled with ½ inch of water to keep the jars from cracking while baking the frittatas.

Bake for 25 to 30 minutes or until the eggs are set and the top is golden brown. Let stand for 5 minutes before serving.

Sometimes, being with your best friends is all the therapy you need.

Unknown

Mexican Potato Frittata

Can you tell breakfast is one of our favorite meals? Use your favorite salsa with this frittata to make a yummy brunch!

1 teaspoon extra-virgin olive oil

¾ pound red-skin potatoes, cut into ½-inch cubes

6 large eggs

1 (12-ounce) jar medium salsa, divided

½ teaspoon salt

¼ teaspoon coarsely ground black pepper

¼ cup shredded sharp Cheddar cheese

1 medium tomato, diced

Preheat the oven to 425 degrees.

Heat the olive oil in a 10-inch nonstick ovenproof skillet over medium-high heat. Add the potatoes and cook, covered, for 10 minutes or until the potatoes are tender and golden brown, stirring occasionally.

Beat the eggs in a medium bowl using a wire whisk or fork. Stir in ¼ cup salsa, salt and pepper. Stir in the cheese. Add the egg mixture to the potatoes. Cook, covered, over medium-heat for 3 minutes or until the egg mixture begins to set around the edges. Remove the cover and place the skillet in the oven. Bake for 4 to 6 minutes or until the frittata is set.

Combine the tomato and remaining salsa in a bowl and mix well. Serve with the frittata.

Spinach and Mushroom Frittata

8 extra-large eggs

2 tablespoons milk

Salt and freshly ground black pepper to taste

Dash of hot sauce

1 large bunch of fresh spinach, washed, drained and chopped

3 tablespoons unsalted butter

4 ounces mushrooms, trimmed and thinly sliced

⅔ cup grated Gruyère or smoked Gouda cheese

Preheat the oven to 400 degrees.

Whisk the eggs vigorously in a bowl. Mix in the milk, salt, pepper and hot sauce.

Sauté the spinach in the butter in an ovenproof skillet over medium-high heat. Add the mushrooms. Reduce the heat to medium. Pour the eggs into the skillet. Let the eggs stand for several seconds. Stir the eggs gently using a heatproof rubber spatula, starting from the center. (This stirring makes the frittata puff up more in the oven.) Lift the edges so the eggs will float to the bottom. When the frittata is half set, add the cheese. Transfer the pan to the oven and bake for 10 minutes or until puffed and golden brown.

Orange Pecan French Toast Casserole

This is a Fab Five favorite! Be sure to serve each slice bottom side up so the yummy pecan mixture is on top! Can be made the night before.

1 cup packed brown sugar

5½ tablespoons butter, melted

2 tablespoons light corn syrup

Nonstick cooking spray

⅓ cup chopped pecans

5 large eggs

½ cup milk

1 cup fresh orange juice

1 teaspoon grated orange peel

3 tablespoons sugar

1 teaspoon ground cinnamon

1 teaspoon vanilla extract

12 (1-inch-thick) slices French bread (about 1 pound)

Combine the brown sugar, butter and corn syrup in a bowl. Pour into a 9x13-inch baking dish sprayed with nonstick cooking spray. Sprinkle the chopped pecans evenly over the sugar mixture.

Combine the eggs, milk, orange juice, orange peel, sugar, cinnamon and vanilla in a bowl and whisk until mixed. Arrange the bread in a single layer over the pecans in the baking dish. Pour the egg mixture over the bread. Cover and chill for 1 hour or up to overnight.

Preheat the oven to 350 degrees.

Turn the bread over carefully. Let stand at room temperature for 20 minutes to absorb the excess egg mixture. Bake for 35 minutes or until lightly browned.

Twisted French Toast

Debbie made this at our favorite B&B in Buffalo Gap, Texas. It is amazing! Needs to chill for 8 hours or overnight.

½ cup unsalted butter

¾ cup packed brown sugar

½ cup chopped pecans

1 tablespoon maple syrup

8 (1-inch-thick) slices day-old French bread

5 eggs

1½ cups half-and-half

1 teaspoon vanilla extract

1 tablespoon orange zest

2 tablespoons Grand Marnier liqueur

¼ teaspoon salt

Melt the butter in a small saucepan over medium heat. Add the brown sugar, pecans and maple syrup. Cook until the sugar is dissolved, stirring constantly. Pour into a 9x13-inch baking dish.

Arrange the bread in a single layer in the baking dish. Whisk the eggs, half-and-half, vanilla, orange zest, liqueur and salt in a bowl. Pour over the bread. Cover and chill for at least 8 hours or overnight.

Preheat the oven to 350 degrees.

Remove the dish from the refrigerator and bring to room temperature.

Bake, uncovered, for 35 to 40 minutes or until puffed and lightly browned. Turn the bread over and broil until browned.

Praline Apple Bread

This would be perfect to serve at your next brunch!

1 cup sugar

8 ounces sour cream

2 eggs

2 teaspoons vanilla extract

2 cups all-purpose flour

2 teaspoons baking powder

½ teaspoon baking soda

½ teaspoon salt

1¼ cups peeled and chopped tart apples

1 cup chopped pecans, divided

4 tablespoons butter

¼ cup packed brown sugar

Preheat the oven to 350 degrees. Grease a 5x9-inch loaf pan.

Beat the sugar, sour cream, eggs and vanilla at low speed in a large mixing bowl until mixed. Beat at medium speed for 2 minutes.

Mix the flour, baking powder, soda and salt in a bowl; add to the sour cream mixture, beating at low speed until mixed. Stir in the apples and ½ cup of the pecans. Pour into the prepared loaf pan. Sprinkle with the remaining pecans and press lightly into the batter.

Bake for 55 to 60 minutes or until a wooden pick inserted into the center comes out clean. Cool in the pan on a wire rack for 10 minutes.

Combine the butter and brown sugar in a small saucepan over medium heat. Cook until the mixture comes to a boil, stirring constantly. Reduce the heat and boil gently for 1 minute.

Remove the bread from the pan and place on the wire rack. Drizzle with the brown sugar mixture. Let stand to cool.

Poppy Seed Bread

Stephanie has been making this bread for years; it's one of her favorites!

BREAD

3 cups all-purpose flour	1½ teaspoons baking powder
2¼ cups sugar	1½ teaspoons vanilla extract
1½ cups milk	1½ teaspoons almond flavoring
1½ cups vegetable oil	1½ teaspoons butter flavoring
3 eggs	1½ tablespoons poppy seeds
1½ teaspoons salt	

ORANGE ICING

¼ cup orange juice	½ teaspoon almond flavoring
½ cup sugar	½ teaspoon butter flavoring
½ teaspoon vanilla extract	

For the Bread, preheat the oven to 350 degrees. Grease and flour two 5x9-inch loaf pans, or 4 or 5 mini loaf pans.

Combine the flour, sugar, milk, vegetable oil, eggs, salt, baking powder, vanilla, almond flavoring, butter flavoring and poppy seeds in a mixing bowl. Beat with an electric mixer for 2 minutes. Pour into the prepared loaf pans. Bake for 1 hour to 1 hour and 15 minutes.

For the Orange Icing, mix the orange juice, sugar, vanilla, almond flavoring and butter flavoring in a bowl.

Cool the bread in the pans on a wire rack for 10 minutes. Remove the bread from the pans and place on the wire rack. Pour the icing over the bread. Let stand to cool.

Steph's Pumpkin Bread

Very simple and easy to prepare in advance for the holidays.
Makes enough to keep one and give one away!

4 cups canned pumpkin purée

1 cup vegetable oil

4 cups sugar

5 cups all-purpose flour

4 teaspoons baking soda

½ teaspoon salt

1 teaspoon ground cinnamon

1 teaspoon ground cloves

2 cups chopped pecans

½ cup golden raisins

1 cup flaked coconut

Preheat the oven to 350 degrees. Grease and flour three 5x9-inch loaf pans.

Combine the pumpkin, vegetable oil and sugar in a bowl and mix well. Sift the flour, baking soda, salt, cinnamon and cloves into a bowl. Add to the pumpkin mixture and mix well. Stir in the pecans, raisins and coconut.

Pour into the prepared loaf pans. Bake for 1 hour. Cool in the pans on a wire rack for 10 minutes. Remove from the pans.

NOTE: This bread freezes well.

Lemon Raspberry Muffins

2 cups all-purpose flour

1 tablespoon baking powder

½ teaspoon salt

¾ cup sugar

1 cup fresh raspberries

2 large eggs, lightly beaten

1 cup half-and-half

½ cup vegetable oil

1 teaspoon lemon extract

Preheat the oven to 425 degrees. Grease and flour muffin cups or line with paper baking cups.

Combine the flour, baking powder, salt, sugar and raspberries in a large bowl. Make a well in the center of the mixture. Mix the eggs, half-and-half, vegetable oil and lemon extract in a bowl. Add to the flour mixture and stir just until moistened. Spoon the batter into the prepared muffin cups, filling the cups three-fourths full. Bake for 20 to 22 minutes. Remove the muffins from the pans and place them on wire racks as soon as they are cool enough to handle.

Mini Pecan Pie Muffins

These are so stinkin' easy! No reason not to make them often for your family.

1 cup packed brown sugar

½ cup all-purpose flour

1 cup chopped pecans

10⅔ tablespoons butter, melted

2 eggs, beaten

Preheat the oven to 350 degrees. Grease and flour miniature muffin cups or line with paper baking cups.

Combine the brown sugar, flour and pecans in a bowl. Combine the butter and eggs in a bowl and mix well. Add to the brown sugar mixture and stir just until moistened. Fill the prepared muffin cups two-thirds full with the batter. Bake for 20 to 25 minutes or until the muffins test done. Remove from the pan immediately to cool.

Spice Pancakes with Fresh Lemon Sauce

The lemon sauce just makes these pancakes! Perfect for a weekend brunch!

FRESH LEMON SAUCE

1 cup sugar

2 tablespoons cornstarch

2 cups water

4 tablespoons butter

2 tablespoons grated lemon peel

¼ cup lemon juice

PANCAKES

3 large eggs, separated

1¾ cups buttermilk

3 tablespoons butter, at room temperature

1 tablespoon sugar

2 teaspoons dark molasses

1½ cups all-purpose flour

2 teaspoons ground ginger

1 teaspoon baking soda

1 teaspoon baking powder

1 teaspoon ground cinnamon

½ teaspoon ground nutmeg

½ teaspoon salt

¼ teaspoon ground cloves

For the Fresh Lemon Sauce, mix the sugar and cornstarch in a 1- to 2-quart saucepan. Stir in the water. Bring to a boil. Boil over high heat for several minutes, stirring constantly. Remove from the heat. Add the butter, lemon peel and lemon juice. Stir until the butter is melted. Keep warm.

For the Pancakes, beat the egg whites at high speed in a deep mixing bowl until distinct moist peaks form. Beat the egg yolks, buttermilk, butter, sugar and molasses in large bowl until blended. Add the flour, ginger, baking soda, baking powder, cinnamon, nutmeg, salt and cloves. Beat until smooth. Add the egg whites and fold gently to blend.

Pour the batter ¼ cup at a time onto a buttered nonstick griddle or in a 12-inch nonstick frying pan over medium-high heat, spacing so the pancakes don't touch. Cook for 2 to 3 minutes or until the tops are full of bubbles. Flip the pancakes over and cook for 1 to 2 minutes or until the bottoms are golden brown. As the pancakes are cooked, stack them on plates, or arrange them slightly overlapping on baking sheets and keep them warm in a 150-degree oven. Serve with the warm Fresh Lemon Sauce.

Killer Pumpkin Pancakes

This is a Fab Five favorite! Serve on a crisp fall morning or for a holiday brunch.

1 cup all-purpose flour

1 cup whole wheat flour

2 teaspoons baking powder

1 teaspoon baking soda

1 teaspoon ground cinnamon

1 teaspoon ground allspice

½ teaspoon ground ginger

½ teaspoon salt

2½ cups milk

1 cup canned pumpkin purée

¼ cup honey

1 egg

2 tablespoons unsalted butter, melted, plus extra for cooking

Mix the all-purpose flour, whole wheat flour, baking powder, baking soda, cinnamon, allspice, ginger, salt, milk, pumpkin, honey, egg and butter in a bowl. Pour the batter ¼ cup at a time onto a buttered nonstick griddle over medium-high heat, spacing so the pancakes don't touch. Cook for 2 to 3 minutes or until the tops are full of bubbles. Flip the pancakes over and cook for 1 to 2 minutes or until the bottoms are golden brown. As the pancakes are cooked, stack them on plates, or arrange them slightly overlapping on baking sheets and keep them warm in a 150-degree oven. Serve with warm maple syrup.

I don't know what it is about food your mother makes for you, especially when it's something that anyone can make—pancakes, meatloaf, tuna salad—but it carries a certain taste of memory.
MITCH ALBOM

Orange Rolls

Kids love these! So good and so easy!

8 ounces cream cheese, softened

¼ cup firmly packed light brown sugar

1½ teaspoons grated orange zest

1 (11-ounce) can refrigerated French bread dough

2 tablespoons sugar

1 tablespoon butter, melted

½ cup powdered sugar

1 tablespoon orange juice

Preheat the oven to 375 degrees. Grease an 8-inch round baking pan lightly. Beat the cream cheese, brown sugar and orange zest at medium speed in a mixing bowl until smooth. Unroll the French bread dough on a lightly floured surface. Spread the cream cheese mixture over the dough, leaving a ¼-inch border. Sprinkle with the sugar. Roll the dough up carefully, starting at one long side. Cut into eleven 1¼-inch slices. Arrange the slices in the prepared baking pan. Brush with the butter. Bake for 25 to 30 minutes or until golden brown. Stir the powdered sugar and the orange juice in a small bowl until smooth. Drizzle over the hot rolls. Serve immediately.

Croissant Breakfast Casserole

6 croissants

Butter for the baking dish

1 (18-ounce) jar orange marmalade

½ cup peach preserves

3 ounces fresh orange juice

1 tablespoon grated orange zest

5 eggs, beaten

1 cup half-and-half

1 teaspoon almond extract

Thin orange slice twists and strawberries for garnish

Cut the croissants lengthwise into halves. Place the bottom halves of the croissants in a buttered baking dish. Mix the orange marmalade, peach preserves, orange juice and orange zest in a bowl. Spoon two-thirds of the marmalade mixture over the croissant bottoms. Place the croissant tops on top of the marmalade mixture. Mix the eggs, half-and-half and almond extract in a bowl. Pour over the croissants. Glaze the croissants with the remaining marmalade mixture. Refrigerate, covered, overnight. Preheat the oven to 350 degrees. Bake the casserole for 25 minutes. Let stand for 5 minutes before serving. Garnish with orange slice twists and strawberries.

Gray's Cream Cheese Yum-Yum

This recipe is from one of our favorite friends! His other version is with Italian pork sausage, tomato and oregano.

1 (8-count) can crescent rolls

8 ounces cream cheese

1 red or green bell pepper, diced

1 tomato, diced

1 tablespoon chopped fresh dill weed

½ tablespoon butter, melted

1 egg, beaten

Preheat the oven to 375 degrees. Unroll the crescent roll dough, making 2 rectangles and pressing the seams to seal. Place the cream cheese on 1 portion of the dough. Sprinkle with the bell pepper, tomato and dill weed. Cover with the remaining dough. Pinch all the seams closed, ensuring the cream cheese is completely enclosed in the dough. Place on a baking sheet. Baste with a mixture of the butter and egg. Bake for 12 to 15 minutes or until golden brown.

Sautéed Fruit

A great alternative to fresh fruit. Wonderful served during the cooler months of the year! We have served it with thinly sliced pound cake.

2 Golden Delicious apples, peeled, cored and cut into thick slices

1 Anjou pear, peeled, cored and cut into thick slices

1½ tablespoons fresh lemon juice

3 tablespoons butter, divided

¼ cup orange marmalade

1 tablespoon Grand Marnier

2 navel oranges, peeled and sectioned

Sprigs of fresh mint leaves for garnish

Toss the apple and pear slices with the lemon juice in a small bowl. Melt 2 tablespoons of the butter in a large skillet. Add the apple and pear slices and sauté over medium-high heat until the apples are tender, stirring gently. Transfer the fruit to a bowl using a slotted spoon. Reduce the heat to low. Add the marmalade, Grand Marnier and remaining butter to the skillet and cook until the marmalade is melted, stirring constantly. Pour the sauce over the fruit. Add the oranges and toss gently. Garnish with sprigs of mint.

Pear, Leek and Gruyère Turnovers

May sound like an odd combination, but it works!

2 tablespoons butter

½ cup chopped leeks

1 (6- to 7-ounce) firm ripe pear, peeled, cored and chopped

1½ teaspoons sugar

Salt and pepper to taste

¾ cup grated Gruyère or smoked Gouda cheese

1½ tablespoons chopped fresh chives

1 (17-ounce) package frozen puff pastry, thawed

1 egg, lightly beaten

Preheat the oven to 400 degrees.

Melt the butter in a large heavy skillet over medium heat. Add the leeks and cook for 1 minute, stirring constantly. Reduce the heat to low; cover and cook for 7 minutes or until the leeks begin to brown, stirring constantly. Stir in the pear and sugar. Increase the heat to medium and sauté for 2 minutes or until any liquid evaporates. Season with salt and pepper. Transfer to a bowl and let stand to cool. Stir in the cheese and chives.

Place the puff pastry sheets on a work surface. Cut 4 rounds from each pastry sheet, using a 4½-inch tartlet pan rim or bowl as a guide. Roll out each pastry round into a 5-inch circle. Spoon a portion of the leek mixture onto half of each pastry round, dividing the mixture equally between the pastries.

Brush the pastry edges with egg. Fold the pastry over the filling, pressing to seal. Press the edges with a fork to seal completely. Brush the turnovers with egg. Pierce the pastry in several places using a wooden pick. Place the turnovers on a baking sheet and chill for 20 minutes. Bake for 18 minutes or until puffed and golden brown. Serve warm.

Arlington, Texas

LEISURELY LUNCHES

If we wake up especially early or especially late, we enjoy preparing a leisurely, satisfying lunch. To us, a tasty soup is the ultimate comfort food that becomes even more interesting when accompanied by a crisp combination salad with noodles or nuts and all things green in between. Add balsamic vinaigrette or a spicy Asian dressing, and the safe and sound becomes a tongue-tingling surprise. Our salad recipes also include enticing fusions of meat or fish for an even heartier way to prepare for the challenges of the day.

Spicy Orange Shrimp Seviche

Great for a light summer lunch served with avocado slices. Can also work as an appetizer.

1 pound large shrimp

½ cup ketchup

¾ cup fresh orange juice

¼ cup fresh lime juice

3 tablespoons fresh lemon juice

2 large garlic cloves, minced

1 jalapeño, seeded and thinly sliced

½ teaspoon dried oregano, crumbled

½ teaspoon freshly ground black pepper

¼ teaspoon ground cumin

¼ teaspoon ground cinnamon

Salt to taste

Hot sauce to taste

1 medium red onion, thinly sliced

1 medium tomato, seeded and cut into ½-inch cubes

½ cup chopped cilantro

Cilantro leaves for garnish

Fill a medium bowl with ice water. Bring a large saucepan of salted water to a boil. Add the shrimp and immediately remove the pan from the heat. Let stand for 2 minutes; drain. Plunge into the ice water. Drain, peel and devein the shrimp; pat dry.

Whisk the ketchup and orange juice in a large bowl. Add the lime juice, lemon juice, garlic, jalapeño, oregano, pepper, cumin and cinnamon. Season generously with salt and hot sauce. Add the shrimp, onion, tomato and chopped cilantro. Cover and refrigerate for at least 8 hours or overnight, stirring once or twice.

Spoon the shrimp and sauce into martini glasses or onto small plates. Garnish with cilantro leaves.

Pimento Cheese Sandwiches

Barbara Arrington's BEST pimento cheese

2½ pounds sharp Cheddar cheese, grated

2½ pounds extra-sharp Cheddar cheese, grated

1 (4-ounce) jar chopped pimentos

¼ cup chopped pecans

4 green onions, chopped

½ cup mayonnaise

Thinly sliced bread

Combine the sharp cheese, extra-sharp cheese, pimentos, pecans, green onions and mayonnaise in a bowl and mix well. Spread over bread.

Amanda's Salad

This recipe is from Jan's daughter-in-law. We ask her to bring this to every family celebration.

BALSAMIC VINAIGRETTE

½ cup extra-virgin olive oil

3 tablespoons balsamic vinegar

1 teaspoon Dijon mustard

1 tablespoon chopped shallot

1 garlic clove, crushed

½ teaspoon sea salt

¼ teaspoon freshly ground black pepper

Process the olive oil, vinegar, mustard, shallot, garlic, sea salt and pepper in a mini food processor or blender until well blended.

SALAD

12 cups finely chopped romaine

4 Roma tomatoes, finely diced

2 medium avocados, chopped

1 cup cooked fresh corn kernels, or 1 cup frozen corn kernels, thawed

¾ cup small blue cheese crumbles

1 Granny Smith apple, chopped

Combine the romaine, tomatoes, avocados, corn, blue cheese and apple in a large bowl. Toss with the Balsamic Vinaigrette.

Baby Blue Salad

BALSAMIC VINAIGRETTE

¼ cup extra-virgin olive oil

2 tablespoons balsamic vinegar

2 teaspoons Dijon mustard

2 teaspoons honey

1 garlic clove, minced

1 shallot, minced

Dash of salt

Dash of ground black pepper

SALAD

1 cup water

¼ cup plus 2 tablespoons sugar, divided

1 cup pecan halves

2 teaspoons chili powder

⅛ teaspoon ground red pepper

12 ounces mixed salad greens

4 ounces crumbled blue cheese

3 oranges, peeled and sectioned

2 cups sliced strawberries

For the Balsamic Vinaigrette, combine the olive oil, balsamic vinegar, mustard, honey, garlic, shallot, salt and black pepper in a jar with a tightfitting lid. Cover and shake well.

For the Salad, combine the water and ¼ cup of the sugar in a small saucepan. Cook over medium heat until the sugar is dissolved, stirring constantly. Remove from the heat. Add the pecans to the syrup; let stand for 10 minutes. Drain the pecans, discarding the syrup.

Preheat the oven to 350 degrees. Line a shallow baking pan with foil. Lightly grease the foil; set aside.

Combine the remaining sugar, chili powder and red pepper in a bowl and mix well. Add the pecans and toss to coat. Spread the pecans in a single layer in the prepared pan. Bake for 10 minutes, stirring once. Let stand to cool in the pan on a wire rack.

Combine the greens and blue cheese in a large salad bowl. Pour the Balsamic Vinaigrette over the greens mixture and toss to coat. Top with the pecans, oranges and strawberries.

Bermuda Salad Bowl

This recipe is from Cindy Schmidt, a fellow foodie!

SALAD

- 1 head of iceberg lettuce, shredded
- 1 head of cauliflower, cut into small pieces
- ½ red onion, chopped
- ½ cup green olives, chopped
- ½ cup blue cheese crumbles

GARLIC HORSERADISH DRESSING

- 2 garlic cloves, minced
- ½ teaspoon salt
- ½ teaspoon pepper
- ½ teaspoon Worcestershire sauce
- 1 tablespoon horseradish sauce
- ½ cup vegetable oil

For the Salad, combine the lettuce, cauliflower, onion, olives and blue cheese in a large bowl.

For the Garlic Horseradish Dressing, whisk the garlic, salt, pepper, Worcestershire sauce, horseradish sauce and vegetable oil in a small bowl.

Pour the Garlic Horseradish Dressing over the salad and toss to mix well. Serve immediately.

Earl's Favorite Wedge Salad

Use as much of each ingredient as you would like.

1 head of iceberg lettuce, cut into wedges

Cherry tomatoes, cut into halves

Red onion, cut into slivers

Chopped cooked bacon

Toasted pecan pieces

Blue cheese crumbles (preferably Maytag)

Briannas Creamy True Blue Cheese Dressing (love all the dressings made by Briannas)

Place lettuce wedges on salad plates. Arrange cherry tomatoes around the lettuce. Sprinkle with onion, bacon, pecans and blue cheese. Pour dressing over the salads.

Cooking well doesn't mean cooking fancy.
JULIA CHILD

Mixed Greens with Apples and Blue Cheese

HONEY LEMON VINAIGRETTE

2 tablespoons sherry wine vinegar

1 tablespoon fresh lemon juice

1 tablespoon honey

¼ teaspoon salt

¼ teaspoon black pepper

⅓ cup extra-virgin olive oil

SALAD

10 cups mixed salad greens

4 ounces blue cheese (or for less pungency, use feta cheese)

3 large Gala apples, cored and cut into ½-inch cubes

2 ribs of celery, sliced

½ red onion, thinly sliced

For the Honey Lemon Vinaigrette, whisk the vinegar, lemon juice, honey, salt and pepper in a medium bowl. Add the olive oil gradually, whisking constantly. Whisk until thick and well blended.

For the Salad, toss the greens, blue cheese, apples, celery and onion in a large bowl until well mixed. Drizzle the Honey Lemon Vinaigrette over the salad and toss to mix. Serve immediately.

Nancy's Apple and Pecan Salad

This is Jan's dear friend Nancy's great recipe! It's ideal for a summer barbecue.

1 tablespoon butter

½ cup pecan halves

1 tablespoon brown sugar

1 (6-ounce) package fresh baby spinach, stems removed

1 large Granny Smith apple, thinly sliced

½ cup crumbled feta cheese

2 tablespoons extra-virgin olive oil

2 tablespoons white or red wine vinegar

Melt the butter in a skillet over low heat. Add the pecans and brown sugar. Cook for 2 to 3 minutes, stirring constantly. Spread on waxed paper to cool.

Place the spinach in a large bowl. Add the pecans, apple, cheese, olive oil and vinegar and toss to mix.

Chicken and Rice Salad

3 cups coarsely chopped cooked chicken

2 tablespoons honey

1 teaspoon salt

2 cups cooked rice

1 pound seedless green grapes, cut lengthwise into halves

1 cup sliced celery

1 small can mandarin oranges

1 (13-ounce) can pineapple chunks, drained

1½ cups slivered almonds

1½ cups mayonnaise

1 tablespoon poppy seeds

Combine the chicken, honey, salt, rice, grapes, celery, mandarin oranges, pineapple, almonds, mayonnaise and poppy seeds in a bowl and mix well. Chill, covered, for several hours or overnight.

Red, White and Green Salad

This is a beautiful and tasty salad. Perfect for the holidays!

CILANTRO DRESSING

¼ cup loosely packed cilantro leaves

4 scallions (dark green tops only), thinly sliced (save the white part)

1 teaspoon seeded and finely chopped jalapeño

2 tablespoons fresh lime juice

¼ teaspoon kosher salt

½ cup extra-virgin olive oil

SALAD

1 avocado, peeled, pitted and cut into bite-size pieces

1 head of butter or Boston lettuce, chopped

12 cherry tomatoes, cut into halves

¼ cup loosely packed cilantro leaves

3 ounces ricotta salata

4 scallions (white parts only), thinly sliced

For the Cilantro Dressing, combine the cilantro, scallions, 1 teaspoon jalapeño, lime juice and salt in a mini food processor or blender; pulse to mix. Add the olive oil gradually, processing constantly and adding additional jalapeño if desired.

For the Salad, mix the avocado with half of the Cilantro Dressing in a small bowl to keep the avocado from browning; set aside.

Place the lettuce in the bottom of a large serving bowl. Add the tomatoes and cilantro. Crumble the cheese over the salad and sprinkle with the scallions. Spoon the avocado onto the center of the salad. Serve the remaining Cilantro Dressing on the side.

Roquefort Pear Salad

RED WINE VINAIGRETTE

⅓ cup extra-virgin olive oil

3 tablespoons red wine vinegar

1½ teaspoons sugar

½ teaspoon prepared mustard

1 garlic clove, chopped

½ teaspoon salt

Freshly ground black pepper to taste

SALAD

½ cup pecan halves

¼ cup sugar

1 head of leaf lettuce, torn into bite-size pieces

3 pears, peeled, cored and chopped

5 ounces Roquefort cheese, crumbled

1 avocado, peeled, pitted and diced

½ cup thinly sliced green onions

For the Red Wine Vinaigrette, whisk the oil, vinegar, sugar, mustard, garlic, salt and pepper in a bowl until well blended.

For the Salad, combine the pecans and sugar in a skillet over medium heat. Cook until the sugar is melted and the pecans are caramelized, stirring constantly. Spread carefully on waxed paper. Let stand to cool. Break into pieces.

Layer the lettuce, pears, cheese, avocado and green onions in a large serving bowl. Pour the Red Wine Vinaigrette over the salad. Sprinkle with the pecans and serve.

Salad with Asparagus and Creamy Garlic Dressing

CREAMY GARLIC DRESSING

4 garlic cloves

1 teaspoon salt

1 teaspoon freshly ground black pepper

½ teaspoon dry mustard

1 teaspoon Dijon mustard

1 large egg

1 tablespoon fresh lemon juice

¼ cup balsamic vinegar

¼ cup extra-virgin olive oil

½ cup vegetable oil

SALAD

3 heads of fresh salad greens, washed and torn into bite-size pieces, or 2 packages of salad greens

1 pound fresh asparagus, blanched and cut into 1½-inch pieces

1 medium zucchini, grated

3 red or yellow bell peppers, roasted, peeled, seeded and chopped, or 1 jar roasted red peppers, well drained and chopped

½ cup sunflower seeds

For the Creamy Garlic Dressing, blend the garlic, salt, pepper, dry mustard, Dijon mustard, egg, lemon juice, vinegar, olive oil and vegetable oil thoroughly in a bowl. Refrigerate until ready to assemble the salad.

For the Salad, combine the greens, asparagus, zucchini, bell peppers and sunflower seeds in a large bowl. Add the Creamy Garlic Dressing and toss to mix.

Tossed Guacamole Salad

SALAD

- 1 package romaine, torn into bite-size pieces
- ¼ cup grated Cheddar cheese
- ¼ cup grated Monterey Jack cheese
- ½ cup sliced green onions
- 8 cherry tomatoes, cut into halves

AVOCADO DRESSING

- 1 avocado, peeled, pitted and mashed
- 1 tablespoon fresh lemon juice
- ½ cup sour cream
- 1 tablespoon extra-virgin olive oil
- 2 to 3 tablespoons picante sauce
- 1 cup crushed corn chips (preferably Chili Cheese Fritos)

For the Salad, combine the romaine, Cheddar cheese, Monterey Jack cheese, green onions and tomatoes in a salad bowl. Cover and refrigerate until serving time.

For the Avocado Dressing, combine the avocado, lemon juice, sour cream, olive oil and picante sauce in a bowl and mix well.

Pour the Avocado Dressing over the salad and sprinkle with the corn chips.

Spinach Salad with Chicken

DIJON VINAIGRETTE

3 tablespoons white wine vinegar

2 tablespoons extra-virgin olive oil

1 tablespoon Dijon mustard

Salt and freshly ground black pepper to taste

SALAD

1 package chopped spinach (about 8 cups)

1 cup halved cherry tomatoes or pear tomatoes

½ cup corn kernels (frozen, canned or cut off the cob)

1½ cups chopped cooked chicken

1 large avocado, sliced

⅓ cup crumbled goat cheese or feta cheese

¼ cup pine nuts, toasted

For the Dijon Vinaigrette, whisk the vinegar, olive oil, Dijon mustard, salt and pepper in a small bowl and mix well.

For the Salad, place the spinach in a large salad bowl. Add the tomatoes, corn, chicken, avocado, cheese and pine nuts. Pour the desired amount of the Dijon Vinaigrette over the salad and toss to mix.

Chinese Chicken Salad

SESAME VINAIGRETTE

¾ cup vegetable oil

¼ cup apple cider vinegar

⅓ cup soy sauce

3 tablespoons dark sesame oil

1 tablespoon honey

2 garlic cloves, minced

1 teaspoon fresh ginger, peeled and grated

1 tablespoon white sesame seeds, toasted

½ cup smooth peanut butter

2 teaspoons kosher salt

1 teaspoon freshly ground black pepper

SALAD

8 split skin-on bone-in chicken breasts

Extra-virgin olive oil

Kosher salt

Freshly ground black pepper

1 pound asparagus, cut diagonally into thirds

2 red bell peppers

4 scallions with green tops, sliced diagonally

2 tablespoons white sesame seeds, toasted

For the Sesame Vinaigrette, whisk the vegetable oil, vinegar, soy sauce, sesame oil, honey, garlic, ginger, sesame seeds, peanut butter, salt and pepper in a bowl until well blended.

For the Salad, preheat the oven to 350 degrees.

Arrange the chicken on a baking pan and rub with olive oil. Sprinkle liberally with salt and pepper. Roast for 35 to 40 minutes or until the chicken is cooked through. Set aside until cool enough to handle.

Shred the chicken into large bite-size pieces, discarding the skin and bones.

Cook the asparagus in a pot of boiling salted water for 3 to 5 minutes or until crisp-tender. Plunge into ice water; drain. Cut the bell peppers into strips about the size of the asparagus pieces. Combine the shredded chicken, asparagus and bell peppers in a large bowl.

Pour the Sesame Vinaigrette over the chicken mixture and toss to mix. Sprinkle with the scallions and sesame seeds. Serve cold or at room temperature.

NOTE: To toast the sesame seeds, place the sesame seeds in a dry sauté pan over medium heat. Cook for 5 minutes or until lightly browned, shaking the pan frequently.

Spicy Thai Chicken Salad

SPICY DRESSING

½ teaspoon finely grated lemon peel, or minced lemongrass

½ teaspoon chili garlic sauce

2 teaspoons roasted peanut oil

3 tablespoons fresh lime juice

2 teaspoons sugar

2 teaspoons fish sauce

½ teaspoon kosher salt

½ teaspoon minced fresh garlic

SALAD

1¼ pounds chicken breast tenders

2 teaspoons chili garlic sauce

1 teaspoon roasted peanut oil

6 cups coarsely chopped romaine

2 cups shredded bok choy

1½ cups thinly sliced green onions

1 cup peeled, seeded and chopped cucumber

1 cup julienned red bell pepper

½ cup chopped cilantro

¼ cup chopped fresh mint

For the Spicy Dressing, whisk the lemon peel, chili garlic sauce, peanut oil, lime juice, sugar, fish sauce, salt and garlic in a small bowl until well blended. Chill until ready to use.

For the Salad, combine the chicken and chili garlic sauce in a large resealable plastic bag. Marinate in the refrigerator for 30 minutes. Heat the peanut oil in a large nonstick skillet over medium-high heat. Add the chicken and sauté for 10 minutes or until cooked through. Let stand to cool.

Combine the romaine, bok choy, green onions, cucumber, bell pepper, cilantro and mint in a large bowl and toss gently to mix. Add the chicken and drizzle with the Spicy Dressing, tossing to coat. Serve.

Tarragon Walnut Chicken Salad

This salad is great served over shredded lettuce or as a sandwich.

4 boneless skinless chicken breast halves

¼ cup mayonnaise

¼ cup sour cream

1 tablespoon tarragon wine vinegar

½ teaspoon salt

⅛ teaspoon freshly ground black pepper

2 tablespoons walnut oil

2 tablespoons chopped fresh tarragon

1 tablespoon chopped fresh chives

1 cup coarsely chopped walnuts

½ cup chopped dried apricots

Arrange the chicken in a large skillet or Dutch oven. Add enough water to cover the chicken. Bring to a boil over medium-high heat. Reduce the heat to low; simmer for 15 minutes or until no longer pink in the center and the juices run clear. Remove the chicken from the liquid; cool. Cut the chicken into ½-inch cubes.

Blend the mayonnaise and sour cream in a small bowl. Stir in the vinegar, salt and pepper. Whisk in the walnut oil until well blended. Stir in the tarragon and chives. Add the walnuts and dried apricots and mix well. Stir in the chicken. Cover and refrigerate for 1 to 2 hours or until well chilled.

Cabo Seafood Cocktail Salad

This is by far a favorite summer salad of ours . . . so easy and healthy!

1½ cups Clamato juice, chilled

¼ cup ketchup

¼ cup fresh lime juice

1 teaspoon Tabasco sauce (optional)

1 teaspoon salt

½ cup finely chopped white onion

¼ cup chopped fresh cilantro

1 firm avocado, peeled, pitted and cut into small chunks

8 ounces lump crabmeat, sorted and flaked

8 ounces shrimp, cooked, peeled and deveined

Combine the Clamato juice, ketchup, lime juice, Tabasco, salt, onion and cilantro in a large bowl and stir to mix. Add the avocado, crabmeat and shrimp and stir gently. Serve over shredded lettuce or in cocktail glasses. May store in the refrigerator for several days.

I followed my heart, and it led me to the fridge.
UNKNOWN

Shrimp and Hearts of Palm Salad

ORANGE PEANUT DRESSING

- ¼ cup extra-virgin olive oil
- 2 tablespoons Thai peanut sauce
- 1 tablespoon orange juice
- 1 teaspoon grated fresh ginger
- 1 teaspoon soy sauce
- 1 garlic clove, minced

SALAD

- 12 ounces cooked shrimp, peeled and deveined
- 4 green onions, chopped
- ¼ cup chopped cilantro
- 1 (14-ounce) can hearts of palm, drained and sliced
- 1 head of Boston lettuce, torn into bite-size pieces

For the Orange Peanut Dressing, combine the olive oil, peanut sauce, orange juice, ginger, soy sauce and garlic in a jar and shake to mix.

For the Salad, combine the shrimp, green onions, cilantro, hearts of palm and lettuce in a large bowl. Shake the Orange Peanut Dressing vigorously and pour over the salad. Toss to mix.

Apricot Almond Turkey Salad

This makes a great sandwich, preferably with pumpernickel bread.

- 1½ cups shredded cooked turkey breast or chicken breasts
- ¼ cup thinly sliced celery
- ¼ cup light mayonnaise
- 2 tablespoons slivered almonds, or nuts of your choice
- 2 tablespoons chopped dried apricots
- 2 tablespoons chopped green onions
- 2 tablespoons raisins
- 2 tablespoons plain yogurt
- ⅛ teaspoon salt

Combine the turkey, celery, mayonnaise, almonds, dried apricots, green onions, raisins, yogurt and salt in a bowl and mix well. Serve as a salad, or place a lettuce leaf on each of 4 pumpernickel bread slices, spread ½ cup turkey salad over the lettuce, top with the remaining bread slices and serve as sandwiches.

Soba and Slaw Salad with Peanut Dressing

PEANUT DRESSING

3 tablespoons soy sauce

3 tablespoons rice vinegar

1 tablespoon canola oil

2½ tablespoons creamy peanut butter

2 teaspoons chili garlic sauce

SALAD

6 ounces uncooked soba (buckwheat) noodles, broken into halves

6 cups shredded red cabbage

2 cups grated carrots

¾ cup thinly sliced green onions, divided

8 ounces shrimp, cooked and coarsely chopped

2 tablespoons chopped dry roasted peanuts

For the Peanut Dressing, combine the soy sauce, vinegar, canola oil, peanut butter and chili garlic sauce in a small bowl; whisk until blended.

For the Salad, cook the noodles according to the package directions, omitting the salt and fat. Rinse with cold water and drain. Combine the noodles, cabbage, carrots, ½ cup green onions and shrimp in a large bowl.

Add the Peanut Dressing to the noodle mixture, tossing gently to coat. Sprinkle with the remaining green onions and peanuts.

Mediterranean Pasta Salad

8 ounces multigrain farfalle

Zest and juice of 1 lemon

2 teaspoons extra-virgin olive oil

1 can artichoke hearts packed in water, drained and chopped

8 ounces fresh part-skim mozzarella cheese, chopped

¼ cup chopped roasted red bell pepper

¼ cup chopped fresh parsley

½ cup frozen peas

Cook the pasta according to the package directions, omitting the salt and fat. Do not drain.

Meanwhile, combine the lemon zest, lemon juice and olive oil in a large bowl; whisk until blended. Add the artichokes, cheese, bell pepper and parsley; toss to mix.

Place the peas in a colander. Drain the pasta in the colander. Shake to drain well; do not rinse. Add the pasta and peas to the artichoke mixture and toss until thoroughly mixed. Serve warm or at room temperature.

Asparagus Salad

LEMON DILL DRESSING

2 tablespoons fresh lemon juice

2 teaspoons chopped fresh dill

1 teaspoon extra-virgin olive oil

¼ teaspoon salt

SALAD

4 cups chopped cooked asparagus, cooked al dente

1 cup chopped plum tomatoes

¼ cup chopped red onion

¼ cup crumbled feta cheese

For the Lemon Dill Dressing, whisk the lemon juice, dill, olive oil and salt in a small bowl until well blended.

For the Salad, combine the asparagus, tomatoes, onion and cheese in a large bowl. Pour the Lemon Dill Dressing over the salad and toss to mix. Serve immediately.

Broccoli, Grape and Pasta Salad

1 cup chopped pecans

8 slices of bacon

8 ounces farfalle

1 pound fresh broccoli

1 cup mayonnaise or yogurt

⅓ cup diced red onion

⅓ cup red wine vinegar

⅓ cup champagne vinegar

¼ teaspoon grated lemon zest

1 teaspoon salt

¼ teaspoon black pepper

2 cups seedless red grapes, cut into halves

Preheat the oven to 350 degrees. Spread the pecans in a single layer in a shallow pan. Bake for 5 to 7 minutes or until lightly toasted and fragrant, stirring halfway through. Set aside.

Increase the oven temperature to 375 degrees. Wipe the pan out and line with foil. Arrange the bacon on the foil and bake for 25 minutes; cool. Crumble the bacon. Set aside.

Cook the pasta according to package directions; drain.

Meanwhile, cut the broccoli florets from the stems and separate florets into small pieces using the tip of a paring knife. Peel away the tough outer layer of the stems and chop stems finely.

Whisk the mayonnaise, onion, red wine vinegar, champagne vinegar, lemon zest, salt and pepper in a large bowl until well blended. Add the broccoli, pasta and grapes and stir to coat. Cover and chill for 3 hours. Stir the bacon and pecans into the salad just before serving.

Broccoli Salad

¾ cup mayonnaise

2 tablespoons vinegar

⅓ cup sugar

3 bunches of broccoli

½ cup dried cranberries

½ cup sunflower seeds

6 slices of bacon, crisp-cooked and crumbled

Mix the mayonnaise, vinegar and sugar in a bowl. Set aside.

Break the broccoli into florets. Combine the broccoli, dried cranberries, sunflower seeds and bacon in a bowl. Toss with the mayonnaise mixture just before serving.

Coleslaw with Dijon Sesame Dressing

1 cup Dijon mustard

3 tablespoons sesame oil

¾ cup rice wine vinegar

¾ cup soy sauce

2 tablespoons sugar

½ teaspoon minced garlic

1 tablespoon freshly grated ginger

¾ cup thinly sliced green onions

¼ cup sesame seeds, toasted

Pinch of cayenne pepper

2 (8-ounce) packages coleslaw mix

For the Dijon Sesame Dressing, combine the Dijon mustard, sesame oil, vinegar, soy sauce, sugar, garlic, ginger, green onions, sesame seeds and cayenne pepper in a bowl and stir until smooth; chill.

Place the coleslaw mix in a bowl. Add the dressing and toss to mix well. Chill until ready to serve.

Chris' Chili Cheese Salad

This is Debbie's friend Chris Slaughter's delicious recipe.
It's yummy!

4 cans whole kernel corn, drained

6 to 8 green onions, chopped

1 green bell pepper, chopped

1 red bell pepper, chopped

1 cup shredded Cheddar cheese

1½ cups mayonnaise

1 package Chili Cheese Fritos

Combine the corn, green onions, green bell pepper, red bell pepper, cheese and mayonnaise in a large bowl and mix well. Stir in the Chili Cheese Fritos just before serving.

Cucumber, Tomato and Mint Salad

10 ounces goat cheese

2 to 4 tomatoes, chopped

4 medium cucumbers, thinly sliced

2 small onions, julienned (Vidalia onions are great if available)

20 mint leaves

½ cup white vinegar

½ cup extra-virgin olive oil

Salt and black pepper to taste

Crumble the goat cheese into a large bowl. Add the tomatoes, cucumbers and onions. Cut the mint leaves chiffonade-style into shreds and add to the tomato mixture. Add the vinegar and olive oil and mix well. Season with salt and pepper. Refrigerate for 1 hour before serving.

Fantastic Cold Green Bean Salad

½ cup extra-virgin olive oil

⅛ cup white wine vinegar

1½ teaspoons lemon juice

¼ teaspoon paprika

¼ teaspoon dry mustard

1½ teaspoons chopped fresh
dill weed, or to taste

½ cup mayonnaise

¼ cup sour cream

¼ cup crumbled blue cheese

2 cans cut green beans

2 bunches of green onions

1 to 2 cucumbers, sliced

Salt and pepper to taste

Combine the olive oil, vinegar, lemon juice, paprika, dry mustard and dill weed in a bowl and whisk until well blended. Add the mayonnaise, sour cream and blue cheese and mix well. Pour over the green beans in a large bowl and mix carefully. Marinate, covered, for 2 hours. Add the green onions and cucumbers and toss to mix. Season with salt and pepper.

Hearts of Palm Salad

DIJON VINAIGRETTE

3 tablespoons extra-virgin
olive oil

3 tablespoons vegetable oil

3 tablespoons wine vinegar

½ teaspoon Dijon mustard

½ teaspoon salt

½ teaspoon freshly ground black
pepper

SALAD

1 (14-ounce) can hearts of palm,
drained and sliced

½ cup chopped red bell pepper

1 (14-ounce) can artichoke
hearts, drained and quartered

10 pimento-stuffed olives

1 head of Boston lettuce

2 hard-cooked eggs, quartered

12 cherry tomatoes, cut into
halves

For the Dijon Vinaigrette, combine the olive oil, vegetable oil, vinegar, Dijon mustard, salt and pepper in a jar with a tightfitting lid. Cover and shake vigorously.

For the Salad, combine the hearts of palm, bell pepper, artichokes, olives, lettuce, eggs and tomatoes in a bowl and toss with the Dijon Vinaigrette.

Southern Okra Salad

8 slices of bacon, crisp-cooked and crumbled

¼ cup apple cider vinegar

¼ cup vegetable oil

2 tablespoons sugar

1 package frozen breaded okra

2 large tomatoes, chopped

1 bunch of green onions, finely chopped

Sprinkle the bacon evenly over the bottom of a shallow serving dish. Combine the vinegar, vegetable oil and sugar in a jar or bowl; shake well or stir and set aside.

Fry the okra according to the package directions. Layer the okra, tomatoes and green onions in the serving dish. Drizzle with the vinegar mixture and toss lightly. Serve immediately.

NOTE: The easiest and best way to cook crispy bacon is to preheat the oven to 375 degrees, line a shallow baking pan with foil, add the bacon in a single layer and bake for 25 minutes.

The Duke's Favorite Salad

Mike Earl, "The Duke," is Diane's husband.

2 tomatoes, cut into wedges

¼ red onion, thinly sliced

1 avocado, coarsely chopped

⅓ bottle Briannas Real French Vinaigrette

¼ cup crumbled feta cheese

Layer the tomatoes, onion and avocado in a shallow dish. Drizzle with the vinaigrette and sprinkle with the cheese. Serve immediately.

NOTE: This is such an easy salad to make and can accompany so many things, such as red meat or pasta, or in the summer, eat it by itself.

Tomato Beet Salad

1 pound small beets, scrubbed

2 pounds tomatoes (preferably heirloom)

1 pint cherry tomatoes

¼ cup crumbled feta cheese

¼ cup fresh cilantro leaves

¼ cup extra-virgin olive oil

Salt and pepper

Preheat the oven to 400 degrees.

Seal the beets in a foil packet. Roast on a rimmed baking sheet for 1 hour and 15 minutes or until tender. Let stand to cool. Rub the beets with a paper towel to remove the skins; slice the beets.

Slice the large tomatoes and cut the cherry tomatoes into halves. Arrange the tomatoes and beets on a platter. Top with the cheese, cilantro and olive oil; season with salt and pepper.

NOTE: Be sure to wear disposable gloves when working with beets, or they will stain your hands red!

Confetti Vegetable Salad

1 pound fresh green beans, cut into ½-inch pieces and blanched

2 ears of corn, blanched for 6 minutes and corn cut off the cob

1 to 2 medium cucumbers, diced

2 large tomatoes, diced

1 bunch of green onions including green tops, chopped

1 to 2 jalapeños, seeded and chopped

Salt and black pepper to taste

1 bunch of cilantro, chopped

2 tablespoons rice wine vinegar

1 tablespoon olive oil

Combine the green beans, corn, cucumbers, tomatoes, green onions, jalapeños, salt, pepper, cilantro, vinegar and olive oil in a large bowl and mix well.

NOTE: If preparing ahead of time, leave the tomatoes and cilantro out until just before serving.

Poppy Seed Fruited Coleslaw

COLESLAW DRESSING

¼ cup sugar

1 tablespoon minced onion

3 tablespoons cider vinegar

1 teaspoon poppy seeds

4 teaspoons canola oil

½ teaspoon dry mustard

¼ teaspoon salt

COLESLAW

½ cup orange sections, chopped

1 cup seedless red grapes, cut into halves

1 (16-ounce) package cabbage and carrot coleslaw

For the Coleslaw Dressing, combine the sugar, onion, vinegar, poppy seeds, canola oil, dry mustard and salt in a bowl and whisk until the sugar is dissolved.

For the Coleslaw, combine the oranges, grapes and coleslaw in a large bowl. Add the Coleslaw Dressing and toss to mix well. Cover and chill for 30 minutes before serving.

Jan's Grape Salad

Great holiday favorite! The Jones' boys love it (especially Stuart). Yum!

2 pounds white grapes

2 pounds purple grapes

8 ounces sour cream

8 ounces cream cheese, softened, or whipped cream cheese

1 teaspoon vanilla extract

1 cup packed brown sugar

1 cup chopped pecans

Cut the white grapes and purple grapes into halves and place in a large bowl. Mix the sour cream, cream cheese and vanilla in a bowl until well blended. Add to the grapes and toss to mix. Spoon into a serving dish. Sprinkle with a mixture of the brown sugar and pecans. Refrigerate for at least 5 hours before serving.

Pink Stuff

Every family has their favorite refrigerated salad. This is ours.

1 (15-ounce) can crushed pineapple in its own juice, well drained

8 ounces frozen whipped topping, thawed

1 (14-ounce) can sweetened condensed milk

1 (21-ounce) can cherry pie filling

½ cup chopped pecans

Combine the pineapple, whipped topping, condensed milk, pie filling and pecans in a bowl and mix well. Chill for several hours to overnight. Best prepared at least 1 day before serving.

Strawberry Pretzel Gelatin Salad

2 cups crushed pretzels

¾ cup butter, melted

1 cup plus 3 tablespoons sugar, divided

8 ounces cream cheese, softened

8 ounces frozen whipped topping, thawed

2 (3-ounce) packages strawberry gelatin

2 cups boiling water

2 (10-ounce) packages frozen strawberries

Preheat the oven to 400 degrees.

Combine the pretzels, butter and 3 tablespoons of the sugar in a bowl and mix well. Press over the bottom of a 9x13-inch baking dish. Bake for 8 to 10 minutes or until firm. Set aside to cool.

Combine the cream cheese and remaining sugar in a large mixing bowl and beat until well mixed. Fold in the whipped topping. Spread over the crust.

Dissolve the gelatin in the boiling water in a bowl. Cut the frozen strawberries into fourths. Stir into the gelatin. Let stand until the gelatin is about the consistency of egg whites. Spread over the cream cheese mixture. Refrigerate until set.

Mexican Soup

- 1 pound ground beef, cooked and drained
- 1 envelope taco seasoning mix
- 2 cups diced tomatoes
- ¼ cup finely chopped jalapeño
- 1 cup chopped onion
- 2 pounds russet potatoes, cubed
- 4 cups water
- 2 tablespoons chicken base
- 1 tablespoon ground cumin
- 1 tablespoon granulated garlic
- 1 (15-ounce) can pinto beans
- 8 ounces Velveeta cheese, cubed

Combine the ground beef, taco seasoning mix, tomatoes, jalapeño, onion, potatoes, water, chicken base, cumin, garlic and beans in a large pot or slow cooker. Cook until the potatoes are tender. Add the cheese and cook until the cheese is melted, stirring occasionally. Serve immediately.

Spicy Vegetable Soup

- 1 pound ground beef
- 1 cup chopped onion
- 2 garlic cloves, pressed
- 1 (30-ounce) jar chunky spaghetti sauce with mushrooms and peppers
- 1 (10-ounce) can beef broth
- 2 cups water
- 1 cup sliced celery
- 1 teaspoon sugar
- 1 teaspoon salt
- ½ teaspoon freshly ground black pepper
- 1 (10-ounce) can diced tomatoes and green chilies
- 1 (16-ounce) package frozen mixed vegetables

Brown the ground beef with the onion and garlic in a large Dutch oven over medium heat, stirring to crumble; drain. Add the spaghetti sauce, broth, water, celery, sugar, salt and pepper. Bring to a boil. Reduce the heat and simmer, covered, for 20 minutes, stirring frequently. Stir in the tomatoes and green chilies and mixed vegetables; return to a boil. Cover and simmer for 10 minutes.

Taco Soup-ed Up

This is quick and yummy! Great for a cold evening!

- 2 pounds ground beef
- 1 medium onion, finely diced
- 2 teaspoons seasoned salt or garlic salt
- ½ teaspoon black pepper
- 2 envelopes taco seasoning mix
- 1 envelope ranch dressing mix
- 1 (28-ounce) can diced tomatoes
- 1 (18-ounce) can tomato juice, or for more spice, add 3 (6-ounce) cans spicy V-8 juice
- 1 (15-ounce) can red kidney beans
- 1 (15-ounce) can pinto beans
- 1 (14-ounce) can yellow hominy

Brown the ground beef with the onion, seasoned salt and pepper in a Dutch oven over medium-high heat; drain. Stir in the taco seasoning mix and ranch dressing mix. Add the tomatoes, tomato juice, kidney beans, pinto beans and hominy and mix well. Bring to a boil. Reduce the heat. Simmer for 20 minutes.

Green Chile Stew

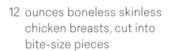

- 12 ounces boneless skinless chicken breasts, cut into bite-size pieces
- 1 medium onion, coarsely chopped
- 2 garlic cloves, minced
- 2 tablespoons olive oil
- 1 (14-ounce) can reduced-sodium chicken broth
- 8 ounces red or white potatoes, cut into ½-inch cubes
- 2 medium carrots, peeled and cut into ½-inch cubes
- 1 (15-ounce) can whole tomatoes, cut up
- ½ cup water
- 1 (4-ounce) can diced green chilies, drained
- 1 teaspoon chili powder
- 1 teaspoon dried basil, crushed
- ¼ teaspoon salt
- ¼ teaspoon ground black pepper

Cook the chicken, onion and garlic in the hot olive oil in a large saucepan until the chicken is browned and the onion is tender; drain. Stir in the broth, potatoes, carrots, undrained tomatoes, water, chilies, chili powder, basil, salt and pepper. Bring to a boil; reduce the heat. Cover and simmer for 30 minutes.

Phyllis' Chicken Chowder

3 medium onions, chopped

½ cup vegetable oil

1 large russet potato, cut into ¼-inch cubes

3 garlic cloves, minced

1 jalapeño, seeded and finely minced

¼ cup all-purpose flour

3 cups chicken broth, divided

2 cups heavy cream or half-and-half

2 plum tomatoes, peeled, seeded and diced

2 cups fresh or frozen corn kernels

1 cup grated Monterey Jack cheese

1 tablespoon chopped fresh parsley

½ can chipotle in adobo sauce, finely minced

1 rotisserie chicken, skinned and shredded

Salt and pepper to taste

Cook the onions in the vegetable oil in a heavy 6-quart pot over medium heat until tender, stirring frequently. Add the potato, garlic and jalapeño and cook for 1 minute, stirring constantly.

Stir in the flour and cook over medium-low heat for 2 minutes, stirring constantly. Whisk in 2 cups of the broth and heavy cream and bring to a boil, stirring constantly. Add the tomatoes, corn, cheese, parsley, chipotle and chicken and simmer, stirring occasionally. Add enough of the remaining broth to thin the soup to desired consistency. Cook for 20 minutes or until the vegetables are tender. Season with salt and pepper.

White Chili

This yummy recipe is from Linda Greenstreet.

2 to 3 pounds chicken or turkey, cooked and chopped

4 (15-ounce) cans Great Northern beans

2 (4-ounce) cans chopped green chilies

1 can chicken broth

1 rib of celery, chopped

1 large onion, chopped

1 medium jar salsa

8 ounces cream cheese

Fritos Scoops

Grated Monterey Jack cheese

Combine the chicken, undrained beans, chilies, broth, celery and onion in a large pot over medium heat. Mix the salsa and cream cheese in a bowl until smooth. Add to the chicken mixture and mix well. Simmer for 15 to 20 minutes, stirring frequently. Serve over Fritos Scoops in soup bowls. Sprinkle with cheese.

Healthy Turkey Tortilla Soup

2 (14-ounce) cans chicken broth

½ cup long-grain white rice

1 teaspoon ground cumin

2 cups cubed cooked turkey

1 (11-ounce) can Mexican-style corn

1 cup thick and chunky salsa

1 tablespoon chopped fresh cilantro

2 tablespoons lime juice

Crisp tortilla strips

Bring the broth, rice and cumin to a boil in a saucepan. Cover and cook over low heat for 20 minutes. Stir in the turkey, corn, salsa, cilantro and lime juice and cook until heated through. Top servings with tortilla strips.

Sicilian Chicken Soup

4 to 5 quarts chicken broth

2 quarts water

1 medium onion, quartered

5 medium carrots, peeled and diced

2 cups sliced celery including leafy tops

5 peppercorns

1 rotisserie chicken

1 (8-ounce) can tomato sauce

1 tablespoon salt

1 tablespoon dried basil

3 chicken bouillon cubes

12 ounces small bowtie or penne pasta, cooked

1 cup freshly shredded Parmesan cheese

Bring the broth and water to a boil in a Dutch oven. Add the onion, carrots, celery and peppercorns and cook until the vegetables are tender, stirring occasionally.

Cut the chicken into bite-size pieces, discarding the skin and bones. Add the chicken, tomato sauce, salt, basil and bouillon cubes to the onion mixture and simmer for 20 minutes, stirring frequently. Ladle over pasta in soup bowls. Sprinkle with cheese.

To feel safe and warm on a cold wet night all you really need is soup.
LAURIE COLWIN

Jalapeño and Cilantro Soup

Rotisserie chicken may be added for a heartier soup.

3 jalapeños, stemmed, seeded and finely diced

½ yellow onion, finely chopped

2 tablespoons corn oil

1 avocado, peeled, pitted and cut into small chunks

1 (16-ounce) can diced tomatoes

8 cups heavy cream

Salt and black pepper to taste

½ teaspoon finely chopped garlic

½ bunch of cilantro, chopped

Sauté the jalapeños and onion in the corn oil in a skillet until the onion is translucent. Add the avocado and undrained tomatoes and bring to a boil. Add the cream, salt, pepper and garlic and simmer until reduced by a fourth. Adjust the seasonings and stir in the cilantro. Serve immediately.

Susan's Lentil Stew

Debbie's sister, Susan, makes this, and it is a meal in itself! If you like it more stew-like, add less broth.

1 small onion, chopped

2 garlic cloves, crushed

3 carrots, peeled and chopped

2 ribs of celery, chopped

3 slices of bacon, chopped

1 cup dry lentils, sorted and rinsed

1 teaspoon dried thyme

3 tablespoons tomato paste

3 to 4 cups chicken broth

Sauté the onion, garlic, carrots, celery and bacon in a skillet until the onion and carrots are tender. Add the lentils, thyme and tomato paste and stir to mix well. Add enough broth to make of the desired consistency. Cook for 30 to 40 minutes or until the lentils are tender, stirring occasionally.

Simple Tomato Basil Soup

Too simple to be this delicious. Great served with grilled cheese sandwiches.

1 (32-ounce) jar tomato basil pasta sauce

2 pints half-and-half

¼ cup chopped fresh basil

Parmesan cheese

Combine the pasta sauce, half-and-half and basil in a saucepan. Cook over low heat until heated through. Sprinkle servings with Parmesan cheese.

Barley and Vegetable Soup

¾ cup medium pearl barley

11 cups vegetable stock, divided

2 tablespoons vegetable oil

1½ cups chopped onions

1 cup chopped carrots

½ cup chopped celery

1 cup thinly sliced mushrooms

Salt to taste

½ bunch of fresh parsley, chopped, for garnish

Combine the barley and 3 cups of the vegetable stock in a saucepan. Bring to a boil over medium heat. Cover and simmer for 1 hour or until the liquid is absorbed.

Meanwhile, heat the vegetable oil in a large pot and add the onions, carrots, celery and mushrooms. Cover and sauté the vegetables for about 5 minutes or just until tender. Add the remaining vegetable stock and simmer, covered, for 30 minutes.

Add the barley and simmer for 5 minutes longer. Add salt to taste and ladle into soup bowls. Garnish servings with parsley.

Cooking with love provides food for the soul.

UNKNOWN

White Bean and Ground Turkey Slow Cooker Chipotle Chili

Nonstick cooking spray

2 pounds ground turkey breast

1 large onion, chopped

2 medium garlic cloves, chopped

32 ounces chicken broth

1 teaspoon ground cumin

1 teaspoon dried oregano

1 teaspoon chipotle chili powder

30 ounce can white beans (cannellini), rinsed and drained

3 tablespoons fresh lime juice

¼ cup coarsely chopped cilantro

Cilantro sprigs for garnish

Coat a large skillet with cooking spray. Cook the ground turkey with the onion and garlic over medium-high heat for about 10 minutes or until the ground turkey is browned, stirring to crumble; drain. Combine the turkey mixture, broth, cumin, oregano, chili powder, beans, lime juice and chopped cilantro in a 3-quart or larger slow cooker. Cover and cook on Low for at least 4 hours. Garnish servings with cilantro sprigs.

Cheesy Jalapeño Soup

3 carrots, peeled and chopped

3 tablespoons butter

1 tablespoon olive oil

1 onion, chopped

2 to 3 jalapeños, or 1 small can green chilies

1 garlic clove, minced

2 to 3 tablespoons all-purpose flour

2 cans chicken broth

½ to ¾ cup half-and-half

8 ounces grated smoked Cheddar cheese

Boil the carrots in water to cover in a small saucepan until crisp-tender. Melt the butter with the olive oil in a skillet over medium-high heat. Sauté the onion, jalapeños, garlic and carrots in the butter mixture until the onions are translucent and the carrots are tender. Add the flour and cook until the flour is light brown, stirring constantly. Stir in the broth. Bring to a boil. Add the half-and-half and stir to mix. Reduce the heat to low and add the cheese. Cook until the cheese is melted, stirring constantly.

Surround yourself with people who make you hungry for life, touch your heart, and nourish your soul.
UNKNOWN

Just Being Silly

Rome, Italy

NIBBLES
AND SIPS

The cocktail hour is always full of promise, a special time to unwind and assess the events of the day with good friends and new acquaintances who also have a story or two to share. Experimenting with new drinks serves as a perfect excuse to gather and relax, and we always try to accompany our cocktails with the kinds of appetizers that offer an unaccustomed combination of interesting flavors and textures. We are pleased to add this compendium of new nibbles and sips to our party repertoire and are confident you will enjoy them, too.

Beer Margaritas

Great poolside drink.

1 can frozen limeade concentrate

1 cup tequila

2 cans beer

Crushed ice

Combine the limeade, tequila and beer in a pitcher and mix well. Pour over ice in margarita glasses to serve.

James' Amaretto or Tequila Margaritas

Jan's friend James loves to make these, and they are the best margaritas!

1 small can frozen limeade concentrate

1 can amaretto or tequila

¼ can Grand Marnier

¼ can Triple Sec

Ice

Combine the limeade, amaretto, Grand Marnier and Triple Sec in a blender. Fill with ice and blend well.

Lemon Drop Martinis

Jan's college friend Cathy is the best at making these!

1½ ounces vodka

½ ounce Triple Sec

1 teaspoon superfine sugar

1½ tablespoons (¾ ounce) lemon juice

Ice cubes

Superfine sugar for garnish

Twisted lemon peel for garnish

Mix the vodka, Triple Sec, sugar and lemon juice in a cocktail shaker half filled with ice. Shake well. Pour strained liquor into a sugar-rimmed glass. Garnish with lemon peel.

> *Pull up a chair. Take a taste. Come join us. Life is so endlessly delicious.*
> RUTH REICHL

Sour Apple Martinis

Ice cubes

2 cups sweet-and-sour mix

1½ cups vodka

1½ cups sweet-and-sour apple schnapps

1 Granny Smith apple, thinly sliced

Fill a 10-cup pitcher halfway with ice. Add the sweet-and-sour mix, vodka and schnapps and stir to mix well. Strain into martini glasses. Push the apple slices onto the rims of the martini glasses.

French 75

Bringing back an old classic. This drink tastes best when served very cold, so make sure the glass and wine are well chilled. Recipe makes one drink.

1 lemon

3 tablespoons (1½ ounces) gin

1 tablespoon (½ ounce) Simple Syrup (recipe below)

1 cup ice cubes

¼ cup (2 ounces) dry sparkling wine, such as brut champagne, chilled

1 blackberry for garnish

Cut the peel from the lemon in a long thin spiral using a zester or paring knife. Juice the lemon. Combine the gin, 1½ tablespoons of the lemon juice and Simple Syrup in a cocktail shaker. Add the ice and shake vigorously for 20 seconds. Strain into a chilled champagne flute and top with sparkling wine. Curl lemon peel around finger to create a twist at least 6 inches long. Garnish the drink with the lemon twist and a blackberry. Serve immediately.

SIMPLE SYRUP

1 part water

2 parts sugar

Bring the water to a boil in a saucepan. Add the sugar and cook until dissolved, stirring constantly. Remove from the heat. Do not allow the syrup to boil for too long or it will be too thick. Let stand to cool completely; the syrup will thicken as it cools.

Hatch Chile Bloody Mary Mix

Great use for those Hatch chiles you froze at the end of the summer!

- ½ cup Hatch chiles, roasted, peeled and seeded
- 46 ounces V-8 juice
- 2 tablespoons chili garlic sauce
- 3 green onions, coarsely chopped
- 1 tablespoon granulated garlic
- 1 tablespoon freshly ground pepper
- 1 tablespoon kosher salt
- Vodka (optional)

Combine the chiles, V-8 juice, chili sauce, green onions, garlic, pepper and salt in a blender and process until puréed. Pour into tall glasses. Add vodka.

Jonnie Delle's Mimosas

- 1 (1-liter) bottle 7UP
- 1 bottle champagne
- 1 pint orange sherbet, softened
- 1 quart orange juice

Combine the 7UP, champagne, orange sherbet and orange juice in a pitcher and mix well. Serve in champagne flutes.

A good friend knows all your stories.
A best friend helped you write them.
UNKNOWN

Maura's Fireball Cider

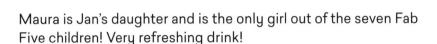

Maura is Jan's daughter and is the only girl out of the seven Fab Five children! Very refreshing drink!

Ice cubes

1½ ounces Fireball cinnamon whiskey

½ ounce peach nectar

½ bottle Angry Orchard Crisp Apple Hard Cider

Place a few ice cubes in a glass. Add the whisky and peach nectar. Fill the glass with the hard cider. Stir and enjoy!

White Sangria

Cut up and freeze the fruit ahead of time.

½ peach, cut up and frozen

½ plum, cut up and frozen

3 strawberries, cut up and frozen

1 tablespoon frozen orange juice concentrate

3 tablespoons superfine sugar

½ cup dry white wine

1 ounce brandy or cognac

1½ cups small ice cubes

Combine the peach, plum, strawberries, orange juice, sugar, wine, brandy and ice in a blender; process until smooth. Pour into a glass and serve.

There comes a time in the day when no matter what the question, the answer is Wine.

UNKNOWN

Fruit Punch

The rum may be omitted for a tasty nonalcoholic punch.

3 cups cranberry juice cocktail

2 cups pineapple juice

2 cups orange juice

1 (1-liter) bottle ginger ale, chilled

¾ to 1 cup light rum

Ice

1 star fruit, cut into ¼-inch slices, for garnish

Combine the cranberry juice, pineapple juice and orange juice in a large bowl. Chill, covered, for up to 8 hours. Stir in the ginger ale and rum just before serving. Serve over ice in glasses. Garnish with the star fruit.

Kahlúa Milk Punch

This is from Diane's friend Beth Ferguson and is a perfect drink for the holidays, especially for anyone who needs an in-law "buffer."

1 cup sugar

½ cup water

3 quarts milk

1 tablespoon vanilla extract

16 ounces bourbon

12 ounces Kahlúa

Combine the sugar and water in a saucepan and bring to a boil. Boil for 5 minutes to make simple syrup. Let stand to cool.

Combine the simple syrup, milk, vanilla, bourbon and Kahlúa in a large bowl and mix well. Freeze overnight. Remove from the freezer 1 hour before serving. Serve while still slushy.

Creamy Peppermint Punch

Great for holiday parties!

1 quart eggnog

1 bottle club soda, chilled

½ gallon peppermint ice cream, softened

Crushed hard peppermint candies for garnish

Combine the eggnog and club soda in a punch bowl and stir to mix. Add the ice cream by spoonfuls and stir. Garnish with peppermint candies.

Chicken Mango Quesadillas

To make this easier, buy pre-seasoned and cooked fajita chicken.

2 cups cooked chicken breasts, cut into strips

2 mangoes, diced

3 tablespoons chopped fresh cilantro

2 jalapeños, seeded and finely diced

2 cups grated Monterey Jack cheese

Lime juice to taste

Salt to taste

6 flour tortillas

6 teaspoons vegetable oil

Combine the chicken, mangoes, cilantro, jalapeños, cheese, lime juice and salt in a medium bowl and toss to mix. Divide the chicken mixture among 3 tortillas. Top with the remaining tortillas. Set aside.

Cook the quesadillas, one at a time, in 2 teaspoons of vegetable oil in a medium skillet over medium heat for 1 minute or until golden brown. Turn the quesadillas over and cook for 1 minute or until the cheese is melted. Remove to a plate and cut into quarters. Serve with fresh cilantro, lime slices, sour cream and salsa.

Chili Crab in Wonton Cups

16 wonton wrappers

2 tablespoons (about) olive oil, divided

⅓ cup minced green onions including green tops

1 (4-ounce) can diced green chilies

6 ounces crabmeat

1 tablespoon prepared mustard

1 tablespoon mayonnaise

½ cup shredded Monterey Jack cheese

Preheat the oven to 350 degrees.

Brush 1 side of each wonton wrapper lightly with olive oil. Center each square oiled side down on a 1¼-inch muffin cup. Press the wrappers to line the cups smoothly; the wrappers will extend above the cups.

Sauté the green onions in ½ teaspoon olive oil in a 6- to 8- inch frying pan over medium-high heat for 1 minute or until limp. Remove from the heat. Stir in the chilies, crabmeat, mustard and mayonnaise.

Divide the crab mixture evenly among the wonton cups. Sprinkle with the cheese. Bake for 8 to 10 minutes or until the wontons are golden brown and crisp. Remove from the muffin cups and serve hot.

Crab Bites

This recipe is from Jan's college friend Tish Corley Deffenbaugh. So good and easy! They need to stay frozen until ready to eat, so they're great to keep around.

1 (5-ounce) jar Kraft Old English cheese spread (find in the Velveeta cheese section)

½ cup butter, softened

1½ tablespoons mayonnaise

½ teaspoon garlic powder

½ teaspoon seasoned salt

1 (6-ounce) can crabmeat, drained well

5 English muffins, split

Combine the cheese, butter, mayonnaise, garlic powder and seasoned salt in a bowl and mix well. Stir in the crabmeat. Arrange the 10 English muffin halves cut sides up on a baking sheet.

Spread the cheese mixture evenly over each muffin half. Cut the muffins into fourths or leave whole. Cover lightly with waxed paper or plastic wrap and freeze for 1 hour or longer. Place the frozen bites in 1-gallon freezer bags and keep frozen until ready to bake.

Preheat the oven to 350 degrees. Bake for 12 minutes.

NOTE: These must be frozen before baking, or they won't turn out as well.

Mushrooms Stuffed with Crab

18 large white or cremini mushrooms

3 tablespoons unsalted butter, divided

2 slices of day-old white bread

2 tablespoons minced celery

2 tablespoons minced red onion

1 tablespoon minced red bell pepper

8 ounces crabmeat, flaked

1 egg, lightly beaten

2 tablespoons mayonnaise

1 teaspoon fresh lemon juice

½ teaspoon Dijon mustard

½ teaspoon Worcestershire sauce

½ teaspoon salt

⅛ teaspoon dried thyme

Remove the caps from the mushrooms, reserving the stems. Melt 2 tablespoons of the butter in a small skillet over medium heat. Dip the mushroom caps in the melted butter and place in a generously buttered 9x13-inch baking pan; set aside.

Preheat the oven to 375 degrees.

Mince the reserved mushroom stems. Cut the crusts from the bread and crumble the bread. Heat the remaining butter in a nonstick skillet over medium heat. Add the mushroom stems, celery, red onion and bell pepper. Cook for 6 minutes or until tender. Remove to a medium bowl. Add the crabmeat, egg, mayonnaise, lemon juice, Dijon mustard, Worcestershire sauce, salt, thyme and crumbled bread and mix well. Fill the mushroom caps with the crab mixture. Bake for 20 minutes or until the mushrooms are tender and the stuffing is heated through. Serve hot.

Bacon-Wrapped Shrimp with Onion Marmalade

ONION MARMALADE

2 large red onions

2 large yellow onions

4 bunches of scallion tops

3 tablespoons olive oil

1½ cups balsamic vinegar

¼ cup packed brown sugar

Salt and pepper to taste

SHRIMP

6 thin slices of smoked bacon,
cut into halves

12 large shrimp (about 1 pound),
peeled with tails intact

For the Onion Marmalade, peel the red onions and yellow onions. Trim the root ends. Stand each onion on its root end and cut through the center of the onion from top to bottom. Cut each half thinly to produce thin, semicircular julienne slices.

Cut the scallion tops into thin slices. Heat the olive oil in a large skillet over medium heat. Add the onions and scallions and toss to coat with the olive oil. Sauté just until the onions are tender. Cover and cook until the onions are wilted.

Increase the heat. Add the vinegar and cook until the vinegar is reduced by half, stirring occasionally. Add the brown sugar, salt and pepper and mix well. Taste the mixture. It should be sweet and sour. Reduce the heat to low and cook for 10 minutes or until the liquid is almost absorbed and the marmalade is thick. Remove from the heat.

For the Shrimp, preheat the oven to 450 degrees.

Wrap the bacon tightly around each shrimp. Arrange the shrimp on a wire rack on a baking sheet. Bake for 5 minutes. Turn over and cook for 5 minutes longer or until the bacon is crisp. Serve the shrimp topped with the Onion Marmalade.

NOTE: Store any extra Onion Marmalade in a jar in the refrigerator. It will keep for up to a week.

Limoncello Shrimp

The limoncello is excellent to sip as you prepare the shrimp!
A Fab Five favorite drink in Tuscany.

¼ cup extra-virgin olive oil

2 garlic cloves, thinly sliced

12 large shrimp, cleaned with tails intact

Juice and finely grated zest of 1 lemon, divided

½ cup limoncello liqueur

Salt and pepper to taste

1 baguette, cut into 12 slices, grilled or toasted

¼ cup chopped green onions

Heat the olive oil in a large sauté pan over medium heat just until smoking. Add the garlic and sauté until light brown. Add the shrimp and cook for 2 to 3 minutes or until bright red. Turn the shrimp over and cook for 1 minute. Add the lemon juice and limoncello and cook for 2 minutes or until the sauce is reduced to about a third. Season with salt and pepper.

Spoon a shrimp onto each toast. Add the green onions to the sauce and swirl for 10 to 15 seconds. Spoon sauce over each canapé. Sprinkle with lemon zest and serve immediately.

NOTE: A crisp green salad goes great with this dish!

Shrimp Taco Bites

So delicious! Very easy to do and can be put together at the last minute.

Nonstick cooking spray

1 teaspoon grated lime zest

2 teaspoons chili powder

1 teaspoon salt, divided

24 large shrimp, peeled and tails removed

1 large avocado, diced

1 tablespoon lime juice

⅓ cup sour cream

1 teaspoon finely minced chipotle peppers in adobo sauce

24 tortilla chip scoops

2 tablespoons freshly chopped cilantro

Preheat the oven to 375 degrees. Spray a large baking sheet with cooking spray; set aside.

Mix the lime zest, chili powder and ½ teaspoon of the salt in a small bowl. Sprinkle over both sides of the shrimp. Arrange the shrimp on the prepared baking sheet. Spray the shrimp with cooking spray. Bake for 5 to 8 minutes or until the shrimp turn pink and curl in on the edges.

Meanwhile, combine the avocado, lime juice and remaining salt in a small bowl. Combine the sour cream and chipotle peppers in a small bowl.

Spoon 1 teaspoon of the avocado mixture onto a tortilla chip. Add ½ teaspoon of the sour cream mixture. Top with a shrimp and place on a serving plate. Repeat with the remaining avocado mixture, sour cream mixture and shrimp. Sprinkle with cilantro.

Shrimp with Mexican Cocktail Sauce

SHRIMP

Nonstick cooking spray

½ cup (scant) all-purpose flour

¼ cup low-fat buttermilk

1 large egg white

1 (5-ounce) bag baked potato chips

1½ pounds medium shrimp, or 24 large shrimp, peeled and deveined

¼ teaspoon salt

¼ teaspoon freshly ground black pepper

MEXICAN COCKTAIL SAUCE

6 tablespoons ketchup

1 tablespoon fresh lime juice

1 tablespoon hot sauce

1 teaspoon prepared horseradish

½ teaspoon grated orange peel

For the Shrimp, preheat the oven to 400 degrees. Spray a baking sheet with nonstick cooking spray.

Place the flour in a shallow dish. Combine the buttermilk and egg white in a medium bowl and stir with a whisk. Place the potato chips in a food processor and process until finely ground. Place in a shallow dish.

Sprinkle the shrimp evenly with the salt and pepper. Coat with flour and dip into the buttermilk mixture. Coat with potato chip crumbs, shaking off any excess. Arrange on the prepared baking sheet. Spray the top of the shrimp lightly with cooking spray. Bake for 10 minutes or until cooked through.

For the Mexican Cocktail Sauce, combine the ketchup, lime juice, hot sauce, horseradish and orange peel in a bowl and mix well.

Serve the shrimp with the Mexican Cocktail Sauce.

Spicy Shrimp Cakes with Corn and Avocado Salsa

You can make these large and serve as an entrée.

CAKES

1 pound medium shrimp, peeled and deveined

Nonstick cooking spray

1 cup finely chopped red bell pepper

1 garlic clove, minced

¼ cup thinly sliced green onions

3 tablespoons mayonnaise

1 tablespoon fresh lime juice

1½ teaspoons hot sauce

½ teaspoon sugar

¼ teaspoon salt

1 large egg

¼ cup finely chopped fresh cilantro

¾ cup panko (Japanese breadcrumbs), divided

CORN AND AVOCADO SALSA

1 cup frozen white corn, thawed

¾ cup diced avocado

¼ cup chopped fresh cilantro

3 tablespoons finely chopped red onion

2 tablespoons finely chopped seeded poblano pepper

1 tablespoon fresh lime juice

¼ teaspoon salt

For the Cakes, place the shrimp in a food processor. Pulse 10 times or until finely chopped. Set aside.

Heat a large nonstick skillet over medium heat. Spray the pan with cooking spray. Add the bell pepper to the pan; sauté for 3 minutes. Add the garlic to the pan and sauté for 1 minute. Remove from the heat.

Place the bell pepper mixture in a large bowl. Add the shrimp, green onions, mayonnaise, lime juice, hot sauce, sugar, salt and egg and mix well. Stir in the cilantro and ¼ cup panko.

Divide the shrimp mixture into 10 equal portions, shaping each portion into a ½-inch-thick patty. Coat both sides of patties with the remaining panko. Chill for at least 1 hour.

Heat a large skillet over medium-high heat. Spray with cooking spray. Add 5 cakes to the pan and cook for 4 minutes per side or until browned. Remove from the pan; cover and keep warm. Repeat the procedure with the remaining cakes.

For the Corn and Avocado Salsa, combine the corn, avocado, cilantro, onion, poblano pepper, lime juice and salt in a bowl and stir gently.

Serve the shrimp cakes immediately with the Corn and Avocado Salsa.

Tex-Mex Shrimp Cocktail

Here's a new twist on an old favorite! The red jalapeño jelly really makes it yummy.

¼ cup red pepper jalapeño jelly

1 tablespoon lime zest

¼ cup fresh lime juice

1 pound peeled cooked large shrimp

1 cup diced mango

½ cup diced red bell pepper

¼ cup chopped fresh cilantro

1 small avocado, diced

Whisk the jalapeño jelly, lime zest and lime juice in a bowl. Pour the mixture into a large resealable plastic freezer bag. Add the shrimp, mango, bell pepper and cilantro, turning to coat. Seal the bag and chill for 4 hours, turning occasionally. Add the avocado right before serving.

Artichoke and Spinach Swirls

2 teaspoons unsalted butter

¼ cup chopped onion

1 garlic clove, minced

2 cups chopped fresh spinach,
blanched and squeezed dry

¾ cup chopped canned artichoke
hearts, drained

½ cup grated Gruyère cheese

¼ cup grated Parmesan cheese
Salt and pepper to taste

1 sheet frozen puff pastry (half of
a 17-ounce package), thawed

1 egg

1 tablespoon water

Preheat the oven to 400 degrees.

Melt the butter in a small skillet over medium heat. Add the onion and garlic.
Cook for 2 to 3 minutes or until tender. Combine the onion mixture, spinach
and artichokes in a medium bowl. Let stand to cool. Stir in the Gruyère cheese
and the Parmesan cheese. Season with salt and pepper.

Unfold the pastry sheet on a lightly floured surface. Spread with the cheese
mixture, leaving a ½-inch border. Combine the egg and water in a small bowl.
Roll up the pastry jelly-roll style, starting at one end. Cut into twenty ½-inch
slices. Arrange the slices, cut sides up, 2 inches apart on baking sheets. Brush
with the egg mixture. Bake for 15 minutes or until golden brown. Serve warm.

Asparagus Toast

8 slices of bacon or ham, crisply
cooked

4 (4-inch) slices of focaccia or
hearty toast

2 pounds (about 24 spears)
asparagus, cooked

2 tablespoons chopped fresh
tarragon

2 tablespoons orange zest

⅔ cup vinaigrette (bottled or
homemade)

4 hard-cooked eggs, finely
chopped

Place 2 slices of the bacon on each piece of focaccia and top with a fourth of
the asparagus.

Combine the tarragon, orange zest and vinaigrette in a bowl and mix well.
Drizzle over the asparagus. Top with the eggs. Serve immediately.

Avocado Rolls

1 cup mashed avocado

1½ cups dry-roasted cashews, chopped

8 ounces cream cheese, softened

½ cup grated sharp Cheddar cheese

2 teaspoons lime juice

1 garlic clove, minced

½ teaspoon Worcestershire sauce

Dash of hot sauce (optional)

Paprika to taste

Combine the avocado, cashews, cream cheese, Cheddar cheese, lime juice, garlic, Worcestershire sauce and hot sauce in a bowl and mix well. Refrigerate, covered, for 30 minutes.

Divide the mixture in half and shape each into a roll. Sprinkle waxed paper with paprika. Coat the rolls with the paprika. Wrap each roll in foil and refrigerate until ready to serve. Slice and serve with crackers. May be made up to 2 days before serving.

Prosciutto and Asparagus Puffs

Parchment paper

24 fresh asparagus spears, trimmed

14 ounces frozen puff pastry, thawed

12 thin slices of prosciutto, cut into halves

1 wheel of Brie, sliced into ¼-inch-thick strips

Preheat the oven to 400 degrees. Line a baking sheet with parchment paper.

Blanch the asparagus in a pan of boiling water for 3 minutes or until al dente. Drain and spread in a single layer on towels to dry. Cut the puff pastry into 24 equal rectangular strips. Place a piece of prosciutto on each strip of pastry. Add a strip of Brie. Press an asparagus spear into each strip of Brie, allowing the asparagus to stick out at either end of the pastry.

Fold the pastry over to create a long thin bundle, pressing the edge to seal. Place seam side down on the prepared baking sheet. Bake for 10 to 12 minutes or until the pastry is puffed and golden brown.

Darla's Mushroom Croustades

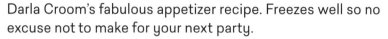

Darla Croom's fabulous appetizer recipe. Freezes well so no excuse not to make for your next party.

2 loaves thinly sliced white bread

Butter, melted

4 tablespoons butter

2 bunches of green onions, finely chopped

1 package sliced mushrooms, finely chopped

2 tablespoons all-purpose flour

1 cup heavy cream

¼ teaspoon red pepper

½ teaspoon salt

1 tablespoon chopped fresh chives

½ teaspoon lemon juice

Grated Parmesan cheese to taste

Preheat the oven to 400 degrees.

Cut the bread into rounds using a 3-inch cookie cutter. Brush each side of the bread with a generous amount of butter using a pastry brush. Press into small muffin cups. Bake for 8 minutes or until brown. Let stand to cool.

Melt 4 tablespoons butter in a skillet and sauté the green onions for 4 minutes. Add the mushrooms and sauté until tender. Add the flour, cream, red pepper, salt, chives and lemon juice; mix well. Add to the bread cups. Bake until heated through. Sprinkle with Parmesan cheese. May be frozen and reheated.

Age and glasses of wine should never be counted.
UNKNOWN

Fran's Cocktail Mushrooms

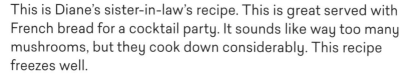

This is Diane's sister-in-law's recipe. This is great served with French bread for a cocktail party. It sounds like way too many mushrooms, but they cook down considerably. This recipe freezes well.

4 pounds button mushrooms

1 quart red wine

2 cups butter

2 cups boiling water

4 chicken bouillon cubes

4 beef bouillon cubes

1½ tablespoons Worcestershire sauce

1 teaspoon dried dill

1 teaspoon garlic powder

Combine the mushrooms, wine, butter, water, chicken bouillon cubes, beef bouillon cubes, Worcestershire sauce, dill and garlic in a large pot. Cook, covered, over low heat for 5 to 6 hours, stirring occasionally. Cook, uncovered, for 3 to 5 hours, stirring occasionally. Serve with French bread.

Finger Sandwiches a la Phyllis

12 slices of white bread, crusts removed

8 ounces cream cheese, softened

12 pickled okra

1 bunch of fresh parsley, chopped

Roll out the bread slices. Spread with a layer of cream cheese. Add a whole pickled okra to each and roll up. Spread cream cheese over the outside of each roll to seal the seam. Sprinkle with fresh parsley.

Grape, Olive and Walnut Medley

We know this recipe sounds a little unusual, but the flavors blend to make a great appetizer.

- 2 to 3 tablespoons olive oil
- 2 cups seedless green grapes
- 2 cups kalamata olives, pitted
- 1 cup walnut halves, broken into halves
- 1 tablespoon herbes de Provence

Preheat the oven to 325 degrees. Drizzle the olive oil over a baking sheet with sides.

Spread the grapes, olives and walnuts on the prepared baking sheet. Sprinkle with the herbes de Provence. Stir until the grapes, olives and walnuts are coated with the olive oil. Bake for 20 to 30 minutes or until the grapes begin to soften. Let stand to cool. Best served at room temperature.

Mediterranean Balsamic Olives

These olives make a great and light appetizer!

- 1 pound green olives, pitted
- 1 pound kalamata olives, pitted
- ¼ cup shaved fresh garlic
- ¼ red onion, slivered
- 1 teaspoon crushed red pepper (optional)
- ½ cup balsamic vinegar
- ¼ cup olive oil

Combine the green olives, kalamata olives, garlic, onion, red pepper, vinegar and olive oil in a bowl and mix well. Serve immediately.

Hot and Spicy Pickles

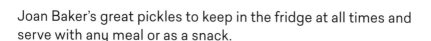

Joan Baker's great pickles to keep in the fridge at all times and serve with any meal or as a snack.

1 (1-quart) jar whole sour pickles

2 cups sugar

1 to 3 garlic cloves, sliced

¼ to ⅓ small bottle hot sauce, or to taste

½ teaspoon red pepper flakes (optional)

Drain the pickles, discarding the juice. Slice the pickles, discarding the ends. Place in a large glass container.

Add the sugar, garlic, hot sauce and red pepper, adjusting the hot sauce if adding the red pepper. Stir gently until mixed.

Cover and let stand at room temperature for 8 to 10 hours or until the sugar has dissolved, stirring occasionally. Ladle the pickles and juice into jars. Chill, tightly covered, for several days, turning the jars upside down and right side up to make sure that the mixture is properly mixed.

Zucchini Appetizers

4 small zucchini, thinly sliced (3 cups)

1 cup Bisquick baking mix

½ cup finely chopped onion

½ cup grated Parmesan cheese

2 tablespoons snipped parsley

½ teaspoon salt

½ teaspoon dried marjoram or oregano

Dash of pepper

1 garlic clove, finely minced

½ cup vegetable oil

4 eggs, lightly beaten

Preheat the oven to 350 degrees. Grease a 9x13-inch baking pan.

Mix the zucchini, baking mix, onion, cheese, parsley, salt, marjoram, pepper, garlic, vegetable oil and egg in a bowl. Spread in the prepared baking pan. Bake for 25 minutes or until golden brown. Cut into 1x2-inch squares and serve.

Barbara's Jalapeño Fudge

This is from Debbie's dear friend Barbara Stone, who is a fabulous cook!

1 pound shredded Cheddar cheese

1 pound shredded Monterey Jack cheese

½ cup all-purpose flour

2 eggs, lightly beaten

1 (5-ounce) can evaporated milk

½ cup pickled jalapeños

Preheat the oven to 350 degrees.

Mix the Cheddar cheese and Monterey Jack cheese in a bowl. Whisk the flour, eggs and evaporated milk in a bowl until blended. Pour over the cheeses and mix well.

Spread the mixture over the bottom of an 11x13-inch metal baking sheet. Sprinkle with the jalapeños. Bake for 30 minutes. Let stand to cool completely. Cut into small squares.

Bronco Busters

This was supposed to be in our first cookbook but didn't make it in for some reason. We love it, so here it is!

1 cup shredded Swiss cheese

¼ cup mayonnaise

1 (4-ounce) can chopped ripe olives

4 green onions, finely chopped

¼ cup crumbled bacon

1 teaspoon Worcestershire sauce

Pepperidge Farm party rye bread

Preheat the oven to 375 degrees.

Combine the cheese, mayonnaise, olives, green onions, bacon and Worcestershire sauce in a bowl and mix well.

Spread about 1 tablespoon of the cheese mixture over each slice of the rye bread. Arrange on a baking sheet. Bake for 10 to 12 minutes. Serve hot.

Bubblin' Cheese Toasts

Similar to the famous Bubble Bread in our first book.

4 (½-inch-thick) diagonally cut slices of French bread or baguette

2 tablespoons unsalted butter, softened

½ teaspoon minced garlic

Pinch of paprika

¼ cup grated Swiss cheese

1 tablespoon grated Parmesan cheese

Preheat the oven to 400 degrees.

Arrange the bread on a baking sheet. Combine the butter, garlic and paprika in a bowl and mix well. Spread a fourth of the mixture over each slice of bread.

Mix the Swiss cheese and Parmesan cheese and sprinkle evenly over the butter mixture. Bake for 10 to 15 minutes or until the bread is crisp and the cheese is bubbly.

Crunchy Cheese Crisps

1 cup finely crushed potato chips

1 cup finely shredded Cheddar cheese

½ cup all-purpose flour

4 tablespoons butter, softened

1 teaspoon Dijon mustard

¼ teaspoon cayenne pepper

Preheat the oven to 350 degrees.

Combine the potato chips, cheese, flour, butter, mustard and cayenne pepper in a bowl and mix well. Shape into ¾-inch balls.

Arrange the balls on a baking sheet and flatten slightly. Bake for 8 to 10 minutes or until golden brown. Remove to a wire rack to cool.

NOTE: Great alone or served with jalapeño or pepper jelly.

Heavenly Cheese Puffs

⅓ cup thawed frozen spinach, squeezed dry

½ cup blue cheese, or for less pungency, use feta cheese

¼ cup bacon bits

2 ounces diced pimento, drained

2 tablespoons ranch salad dressing

1 sheet frozen puff pastry, thawed

Preheat the oven to 400 degrees.

Combine the spinach, cheese, bacon bits, pimento and ranch dressing in a medium bowl. Stir until well blended. Set aside.

Cut the puff pastry into twenty-five 2x2-inch squares. Spoon 2 teaspoons of the cheese mixture onto the center of each square.

Transfer the squares to a baking sheet and bake for 20 minutes or until the pastry is golden brown. Remove from the oven and serve hot or at room temperature.

NOTE: You may cook the bacon yourself or purchase cooked bacon bits.

Creamy White Bean Dip

1 (15-ounce) can cannellini (white kidney beans), drained

1½ tablespoons fresh lemon juice

1½ tablespoons extra-virgin olive oil

1 large garlic clove, peeled

¾ teaspoon ground cumin

Salt and pepper to taste

1 tablespoon chopped fresh mint

1 tablespoon chopped fresh dill

1 teaspoon grated lemon peel

Purée the beans, lemon juice, olive oil, garlic and cumin in a food processor until smooth. Season with salt and pepper. Transfer the dip to a small bowl. Mix the mint, dill and lemon peel in a small dish and sprinkle over the dip. Serve with tortilla chips.

NOTE: The dip can be prepared 1 day ahead. Cover and refrigerate. Sprinkle with the mint mixture just before serving.

Josefinas (Toast with Chili Cheese)

1 (8-ounce) baguette

1 cup shredded Monterey Jack cheese

2 (4-ounce) cans diced green chilies

½ cup minced sweet onion

½ cup sour cream

3 garlic cloves, peeled and coarsely chopped

¼ teaspoon paprika

Preheat the broiler.

Cut the baguette horizontally into halves. Mix the cheese, chilies, onion, sour cream, garlic and paprika in a bowl. Spread the mixture evenly over the cut sides of the baguette; dust lightly with additional paprika. Place the bread cheese side up on a 14x17-inch baking sheet.

Broil 4 inches from the heat source for 6 minutes or until the topping is puffy and lightly browned.

NOTE: For appetizers, cut into 1¼- to 1½-inch squares. To serve with a meal, cut each slice into 3 or 4 sections. Serve warm.

Marinated Bocconcini

½ cup finely diced roasted red peppers

⅓ cup chopped fresh basil

¼ teaspoon crushed red pepper flakes

3 garlic cloves, chopped

¾ cup extra-virgin olive oil

12 ounces baby mozzarella balls

Combine the red peppers, basil, red pepper, garlic, olive oil and cheese in a bowl and mix gently. Marinate, covered, in the refrigerator for at least 4 hours (best if overnight). Serve with wooden picks.

Chicken Enchilada Dip

This recipe was shared by one of Jan's college friends at a reunion. Yummy! Serves lots!

- 1 pound chopped cooked chicken breast (canned chicken works fine)
- 2 (8-ounce) packages cream cheese, softened
- 2 (4-ounce) cans chopped green chilies
- 1 (8-ounce) can or jar diced jalapeños (for less heat, use 4-ounce can)
- 1 pound sharp Cheddar cheese, shredded
- 1 cup mayonnaise
- 1 cup sour cream
- 1 yellow onion, chopped

Preheat the oven to 350 degrees.

Mix the chicken, cream cheese, green chilies, jalapeños, cheese, mayonnaise, sour cream and onion in a bowl. Spoon into a 9x13-inch baking pan. Bake for 30 minutes or until warm and lightly browned. Serve with tortilla chips or crackers.

NOTE: You aren't actually cooking this; you're just melting all the yummy ingredients together. Recipe can be cut in half. Also can make ahead and freeze before baking.

Corn Dip

Easy peasy but always a hit.

- 1 jar corn relish
- 16 ounces sour cream
- 2 cups shredded Cheddar or Colby Jack cheese

Mix the corn relish, sour cream and cheese in a medium bowl. Serve with Fritos Scoops or crackers.

NOTE: Cherith Valley Gardens Hot 'n Spicy Corn Relish is one of our favorite corn relishes, but other brands will work.

Debbie's Fiesta-in-your-Mouth Dip

I love to make this for guests. It's a little spicy, but you can leave out some of the jalapeños. It's best to make this yummy dip a day ahead; cover and refrigerate in an airtight container.

- 8 ounces cream cheese, softened
- ⅔ cup sour cream
- ⅓ cup mayonnaise
- 1 tablespoon finely chopped canned chipotle peppers in adobo sauce
- 2 teaspoons chili powder
- 2 cups chopped cooked chicken
- 2 cups (8 ounces) shredded Colby Jack cheese
- 1 (4-ounce) can chopped green chilies
- 2 jalapeños, seeded and minced
- ¼ cup chopped fresh cilantro

Preheat the oven to 350 degrees. Grease an 8-inch square baking dish lightly.

Combine the cream cheese, sour cream, mayonnaise, chipotle peppers and chili powder in a large bowl and stir until smooth. Stir in the chicken, cheese, chilies, jalapeños and cilantro until blended. Spoon into the prepared baking dish.

Bake for 30 minutes or until bubbly. Serve with any chips of your choice and enjoy!

Olive Dip

This recipe is from our dear friend Jonnie Delle Cogdell. This is an oldie but goodie! This will keep in the refrigerator for a while and is a great, easy appetizer. Actually very addicting!

- 6 ounces cream cheese, softened
- ½ cup mayonnaise
- 1 cup chopped green olives
- Dash of ground pepper
- ½ cup chopped pecans

Combine the cream cheese and mayonnaise in a medium bowl and mix thoroughly. Add the olives, pepper and pecans and stir to mix. Serve with crackers of your choice.

Zesty Crab and Artichoke Dip

This is a great low-fat party dish!

Nonstick cooking spray

1 large green bell pepper, chopped

2 (14-ounce) cans artichoke hearts, drained and finely chopped

1 cup fat-free mayonnaise

1 cup fat-free plain yogurt

⅔ cup grated Parmesan cheese

½ cup thinly sliced scallions

½ cup chopped roasted sweet red peppers, drained

5 teaspoons lemon juice

4 teaspoons Worcestershire sauce

1 tablespoon seeded and finely chopped pickled jalapeño

¼ teaspoon celery seeds

1 pound lump crabmeat, picked over and flaked

¼ cup sliced almonds (optional)

Spray a small skillet with cooking spray. Add the green pepper. Cook over medium heat for 3 minutes or until tender, stirring constantly; let stand to cool.

Preheat the oven to 375 degrees. Spray an 8x8-inch baking pan with cooking spray.

Combine the cooked green pepper, artichoke hearts, mayonnaise, yogurt, cheese, scallions, red peppers, lemon juice, Worcestershire sauce, jalapeño and celery seeds in a large bowl and mix well. Stir in the crabmeat gently. Spoon into the prepared baking pan. Sprinkle with the almonds. Bake for 30 to 35 minutes or until golden brown and bubbly. Serve with crackers or baguettes.

Spicy Spinach Cheese Dip

1 tablespoon canola oil

¼ cup diced onion

½ teaspoon salt

½ teaspoon pepper

½ teaspoon granulated garlic

½ cup plus 1 tablespoon
half-and-half

½ tablespoon dry sherry

1½ teaspoons lemon juice

8 ounces cream cheese,
softened

½ pound pepper Jack cheese

6 ounces spinach, chopped

1 tomato, chopped

⅓ cup roasted red pepper,
drained and sliced

Heat the canola oil in a skillet. Sauté the onion, salt, pepper and garlic in
the oil. Add the half-and-half, sherry and lemon juice and mix well. Bring
to a simmer.

Add the cream cheese and pepper Jack cheese to the onion mixture. Cook
until the cheese is melted, stirring constantly. Add the spinach, tomato and
red pepper. Serve with your favorite crackers or tortilla chips.

Spinach Queso

You can reduce the fat in this recipe by using low-fat or fat-free
half-and-half.

4½ pounds cream cheese,
softened

4 cups salsa

3 cups half-and-half

1½ boxes chopped spinach

1 tablespoon garlic

1 tablespoon chopped onion

2 teaspoons cayenne pepper

2 teaspoons salt

Microwave the cream cheese, salsa and half-and-half in a microwave-safe
bowl in 30-second intervals until creamy, stirring at each interval. Add the
spinach, garlic, onion, cayenne pepper and salt and mix well. Serve with your
favorite chips.

Kerri's Salsa

Diane and Mike's daughter, Kerri, makes this salsa when tomatoes are ripe for the pickin'.

2 tomatoes	2 garlic cloves
½ onion	Juice of ½ lime
1 tablespoon cilantro	½ tomatillo
½ basil leaf	1 jalapeño, stemmed and seeded

Process the tomatoes, onion, cilantro, basil, garlic, lime juice, tomatillo and jalapeño in a food processor until of the desired consistency.

NOTE: You can chop the ingredients by hand if desired.

We didn't realize we were making memories;
we just knew we were having fun.
Unknown

Krazy Krunch

A Fab Five tradition for road trips.

2 quarts popped popcorn

1⅓ cups pecan halves

⅔ cup whole or slivered almonds

1⅓ cups sugar

1 cup butter

½ cup white corn syrup

1 teaspoon vanilla extract

Spread the popcorn, pecans and almonds on a greased baking sheet.

Combine the sugar, butter and corn syrup in a saucepan. Bring to a boil over medium heat, stirring constantly.

Boil the sugar mixture until a candy thermometer inserted into the mixture reaches 300 to 310 degrees, hard-crack stage, stirring frequently. Remove from the heat and stir in the vanilla.

Pour over the popcorn mixture and stir to coat well. Spread in a single layer. Let stand until set. Break into small pieces and store in an airtight container.

New York, New York

THE MAIN EVENT

Entertaining with a sit-down dinner has always been our specialty. We began our friendship preparing elaborate feasts and still enjoy cooking grand meals together, served at elaborately set tables with wine pairings accompanying every course. Over the past fifteen years, we have collected a number of fabulous recipes to prepare for special evening meals. We offer you this eclectic selection of choices for casual barbecues or elegant dinner parties to share with family and friends.

Beef Tenderloin with Onion Sauce

Expensive, yes, but it is all usable protein and as a general rule, you'll eat less.

1 (3½-pound) trimmed beef tenderloin

1½ teaspoons salt, divided

1 teaspoon pepper, divided

2 tablespoons canola oil

3 tablespoons butter

3 large yellow onions, sliced and separated into rings

3 large purple onions, sliced and separated into rings

2 bunches of green onions, chopped

6 shallots, chopped

5 garlic cloves, minced

½ cup cognac

½ cup beef broth

Sprinkle the tenderloin with ½ teaspoon of the salt and ½ teaspoon of the pepper. Brown the tenderloin on all sides in the canola oil in a heavy roasting pan or ovenproof Dutch oven. Remove the tenderloin, reserving the drippings in the pan.

Preheat the oven to 400 degrees.

Add the butter to the drippings and cook over medium-high heat until the butter is melted. Add the yellow onions and purple onions and sauté for 5 minutes. Add the green onions, shallots and garlic and sauté for 10 minutes. Stir in the cognac and broth. Cook over high heat for about 5 minutes or until the liquid evaporates, stirring constantly. Place the tenderloin on top of the onion mixture.

Bake, covered, for 30 to 40 minutes or until a meat thermometer inserted into the thickest portion of the tenderloin registers 125 degrees for medium-rare. Remove the tenderloin from the roasting pan, reserving the onion mixture in the pan. Cover the tenderloin loosely and let stand for 10 minutes.

Cook the onion mixture over medium heat for 3 to 5 minutes or until the liquid evaporates, stirring constantly. Stir in the remaining salt and pepper. Serve with the sliced tenderloin.

The Juiciest Roast Tenderloin

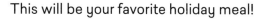

This will be your favorite holiday meal!

- 1 (6- to 8-pound) beef tenderloin, silver skin removed
- 2 teaspoons salt
- 1 teaspoon ground black pepper
- 2 tablespoons dried thyme
- ½ cup salted butter, at room temperature
- 2 tablespoons finely minced garlic
- 3 tablespoons finely chopped shallots

Preheat the oven to broil.

Rub both sides of the tenderloin generously with the salt, pepper and thyme.

Combine the butter, garlic and shallots in a small bowl and mash with a fork. Place the tenderloin in a metal baking pan and rub the butter mixture generously over the top of the tenderloin. Place the baking pan on the middle rack of the oven and broil the tenderloin for 5 minutes.

Reduce the oven temperature to 400 degrees. Roast the tenderloin for 17 minutes.

Preheat the oven to broil and broil the tenderloin for 2 minutes. Remove from the oven. Let stand for 12 to 15 minutes before slicing.

NOTE: Good either warm or cold!

My doctor told me I had to stop throwing intimate dinners for four unless there are three other people.
ORSON WELLS

Blue Cheese–Crusted Steak with Red Wine Sauce

The perfect combination!

4 tablespoons butter, divided

3 garlic cloves, chopped

1 large shallot, chopped

1 tablespoon chopped fresh thyme

¾ cup low-sodium beef broth

½ cup dry red wine

½ cup coarsely crumbled blue cheese (about 2 ounces)

¼ cup panko (Japanese breadcrumbs)

1 tablespoon chopped fresh parsley

4 (1-inch-thick) filet mignon steaks (about 6 to 8 ounces each)

Salt and pepper to taste

Melt 1 tablespoon of the butter in a medium heavy skillet over medium-high heat. Add the garlic, shallot and thyme. Sauté for 5 minutes or until the shallot is tender. Add the broth and wine. Boil for 12 minutes or until the sauce is reduced to ½ cup. Set the sauce aside.

Blend the cheese, panko and parsley in a small bowl, coating the cheese evenly with the panko. (The sauce and cheese mixtures can be made 1 day ahead. Cover separately and chill).

Preheat the broiler. Melt 2 tablespoons of the butter in a large heavy skillet over medium-high heat. Sprinkle the steaks with salt and pepper. Add the steaks to the skillet and cook for 5 minutes per side for medium-rare, or to the desired doneness. Transfer the steaks to a rimmed baking sheet, reserving the drippings in the skillet. Press equal amounts of the cheese mixture onto the tops of the steaks. Broil for 2 minutes or until the cheese browns. Transfer the steaks to plates.

Add the sauce to the reserved drippings in the large skillet. Bring to a boil, scraping up any browned bits. Boil for 2 minutes. Whisk in the remaining butter. Season with salt and pepper. Spoon sauce around the steaks and serve.

> *The only time to eat diet food is while you're waiting for the steak to cook.*
> JULIA CHILD

Rib Eye Steaks with Herbed Compound Butter

The marbling of the fat in this cut of steak makes this very good for slow roasting as well as cooking on the grill.

1 tablespoon kosher salt

1 tablespoon freshly ground black pepper

2 teaspoons onion powder

1 teaspoon dried dill seeds

Grated zest of ½ orange

2 garlic cloves, finely chopped

2 marbled bone-in rib eye steaks

Combine the salt, pepper, onion powder and dill in a bowl and mix well. Add the orange zest and garlic and mix well to make a rub. Rub the seasoning over both sides of each steak. Let the steaks stand for at least 20 minutes.

Preheat the grill to 450 degrees for a great sear.

Grill the steaks for 4 to 6 minutes per side for medium-rare or until cooked to the desired degree of doneness. Remove the steaks from the grill. Let stand for 5 to 10 minutes before serving. Top each steak with a slice of Herbed Compound Butter and serve.

Herbed Compound Butter

This butter would also be good on bread or muffins!

½ cup butter, at room temperature

2 garlic cloves, crushed

2 tablespoons chopped fresh parsley

1 tablespoon chopped fresh chives

1 teaspoon chopped fresh thyme

Pinch of kosher salt

Combine the butter, garlic, parsley, chives, thyme and salt in a bowl and mix thoroughly using a spatula. Place on a sheet of waxed paper.

Roll the butter mixture into a cylindrical shape working with the waxed paper. Twist the edges of the waxed paper and chill the butter until firm. Store any unused compound butter in the refrigerator.

Cowboy Pot Roast

This is a slow cooker recipe. Browning the meat before slow cooking enhances both the appearance and flavor of the meat.

1 (14-ounce) can petite diced tomatoes, drained

1 (10-ounce) can diced tomatoes and green chilies (do not drain)

1 onion, cut into 8 wedges

1 tablespoon chili powder

1½ teaspoons salt, divided

1½ teaspoons pepper, divided

1 (2- to 3-pound) eye of round roast, trimmed

2 tablespoons vegetable oil

2 (16-ounce) cans pinto beans, drained

1 (15-ounce) can black beans, drained

Pickled jalapeños (optional)

Combine the petite tomatoes, tomatoes and green chilies, onion, chili powder, 1 teaspoon of the salt and 1 teaspoon of the pepper in a medium bowl and mix well.

Sprinkle the roast evenly with the remaining salt and pepper. Brown the roast on all sides in the vegetable oil in a large Dutch oven over medium-high heat. Transfer the roast to a slow cooker. Pour the tomato mixture over the roast. Cover and cook on High for 5 to 6 hours or until the meat shreds easily with a fork.

Remove the roast from the slow cooker and cut into large chunks; keep warm.

Skim the fat from the juices in the slow cooker. Mash 1½ cans (about 2¾ cups) of the pinto beans and add to the slow cooker, stirring until mixed. Stir in the black beans and the remaining pinto beans. Add the roast back to the slow cooker; cover and cook on High for 20 to 25 minutes longer. Top each serving with pickled jalapeños.

Beef Tips in Red Wine Sauce

2 cups 1-inch sirloin tip pieces

2 teaspoons olive oil

1 yellow onion, diced

2 cups sliced mushrooms

1 garlic clove, crushed

1 tablespoon all-purpose flour

½ teaspoon dried thyme

¼ teaspoon black pepper

⅓ teaspoon ground nutmeg

½ cup dry red wine

½ cup beef broth

3 cups egg noodles

2 tablespoons chopped fresh parsley

Brown the beef in the olive oil in a 12-inch nonstick skillet over medium heat, turning frequently to ensure even browning. Add the onion and cook for 2 to 3 minutes, stirring frequently. Add the mushrooms and garlic and reduce the heat to medium-low. Cook for 5 minutes or until the mushrooms are brown, stirring occasionally.

Combine the flour, thyme, pepper and nutmeg in a small dish. Sprinkle evenly over the beef mixture, stirring well. Cook for 1 minute, stirring constantly and allowing the flour mixture to brown in the pan. Do not allow the flour mixture to burn.

Add the red wine and beef broth. Cook until the liquid comes to a boil and thickens slightly, stirring constantly. Reduce the heat to low. Cover loosely and simmer for 20 minutes. The sauce will continue to thicken. If the sauce becomes too thick, add a few tablespoons of water or beef broth.

Meanwhile, cook the noodles according to the package directions; drain. Add the noodles and parsley to the beef mixture and cook just until heated through.

Diane's Brisket Tacos

This is a great way to serve a crowd. Put it in the oven first thing in the morning, and it will be great by dinnertime.

1 beef brisket

Knorr Swiss Caldo de Res seasoning to taste

Salt and pepper to taste

1 onion, chopped

¼ cup water

2 cans Hatch green chile enchilada sauce

Diced white onions

Diced tomatoes

Chopped cilantro

Shredded cheese

Flour or corn tortillas

Preheat the oven to 325 degrees. Season the brisket liberally with the Caldo de Res, salt and pepper. Wrap the brisket very tightly in aluminum foil, adding the onion and water before completely sealing. Place inside a large glass baking dish.

Bake for 5 to 6 hours or until the brisket is very tender and shreds easily. Remove the brisket from the foil. Drain well and place directly in the baking dish. Shred the brisket using two forks.

Reduce the oven temperature to 300 degrees. Add the enchilada sauce to the brisket and mix thoroughly. Cover with foil and return to the oven. Cook for 1½ to 2 hours longer.

Combine the white onions, tomatoes, cilantro and cheese in a bowl and mix well. Spoon a generous amount of the shredded brisket onto each tortilla. Top with the onion mixture. Fold the tortilla to enclose the filling.

Serve with brown rice or Spanish rice and black beans or pinto beans.

Jan's Birthday Short Ribs

We serve these with mashed potatoes and a great salad.

8 to 10 beef short ribs

Kosher salt and pepper to taste

¼ cup all-purpose flour

6 slices of pancetta, diced

1 tablespoon olive oil

1 tablespoon butter

1 medium onion, diced

3 carrots, diced

2 shallots, peeled and finely diced

2 cups red wine

2 cups beef broth

1 teaspoon kosher salt to taste

Freshly ground black pepper to taste

2 sprigs of thyme

2 sprigs of rosemary

Preheat the oven to 350 degrees. Season the ribs with salt and pepper and coat with the flour. Set aside.

Cook the pancetta in a large Dutch oven over medium heat until crispy. Remove to a plate, reserving the drippings. Set aside.

Add the olive oil and butter to the drippings and increase the heat to high. Brown the ribs for about 45 seconds per side. Remove to a plate and set aside. Reduce the heat to medium. Add the onion, carrots and shallots to the pan and sauté for 2 minutes. Pour in the wine and scrape up any browned bits. Bring to a boil and cook for 2 minutes. Add the broth, salt and pepper. Add the ribs to the liquid; the ribs should be almost completely covered. Add the thyme and rosemary.

Bake, covered, for 2 hours. Reduce the heat to 325 degrees and bake for 30 to 45 minutes longer. Let stand, covered, for at least 20 minutes. Skim the fat from the top of the liquid before serving the ribs.

Provolone Italian Meatloaf

1 cup boiling water

½ cup sun-dried tomatoes, packed without oil

Nonstick cooking spray

½ cup plus ⅓ cup ketchup, divided

1 cup seasoned breadcrumbs

1 cup finely diced onion

¾ cup coarsely chopped fresh basil

½ cup shredded sharp provolone cheese

2 large eggs

2 garlic cloves, minced

1 pound ground round

½ teaspoon oregano

1 teaspoon salt

1 teaspoon pepper

Combine the boiling water and sun-dried tomatoes in a bowl. Let stand for 30 minutes or until the tomatoes are soft. Drain and finely chop the tomatoes.

Preheat the oven to 350 degrees. Spray a baking pan with cooking spray.

Combine ½ cup of the ketchup, breadcrumbs, onion, basil, cheese, eggs, garlic, ground round, oregano, salt and pepper in a large bowl and mix well. Add the tomatoes and mix well. Shape the mixture into a 5x9-inch loaf and place in the prepared pan. Spread the remaining ketchup over the meat loaf.

Bake for 1 hour. Let stand for 10 minutes before slicing.

One cannot think well, love well, sleep well if one has not dined well.

VIRGINIA WOOLF

Reba's Brisket Enchiladas

Reba is Phyllis' sister-in-law.

ENCHILADAS

- 3 to 5 pounds sliced precooked beef brisket, chopped
- 2 cups shredded sharp Cheddar cheese
- ½ teaspoon ground cumin
- 2 cans chopped green chilies
- Pepper to taste
- Tortillas
- Corn oil or olive oil

TOPPING

- 1 can beef broth
- 1 can beef consommé
- 1 tablespoon chili powder
- 1 can chopped green chilies
- ½ teaspoon ground cumin
- 2 cups shredded sharp Cheddar cheese
- 1 jar salsa

Preheat the oven to 375 degrees. Grease a 9x13-inch casserole dish.

For the Enchiladas, combine the brisket, cheese, cumin, chilies and pepper in a bowl; mix well. Heat the tortillas in a small amount of corn oil in a small skillet over medium-low heat. Spoon a portion of the brisket mixture onto each tortilla and roll the tortilla to enclose the filling. Place each tortilla seam down in the prepared casserole dish.

For the Topping, combine the beef broth, beef consommé, chili powder, green chilies, cumin, cheese and salsa in a bowl and mix well.

Pour the Topping over the Enchiladas and bake for 30 to 40 minutes or until hot and bubbly.

Roasted Pork Tenderloin

This will be your go-to recipe for pork tenderloin!

½ cup olive oil

⅓ cup soy sauce

¼ cup red wine vinegar

Juice of 1 lemon

1 to 2 tablespoons Worcestershire sauce

1 to 2 tablespoons finely chopped fresh parsley

2 teaspoons dry mustard

Freshly cracked black pepper to taste

4 garlic cloves, peeled and minced

1 (1-pound) pork tenderloin, silver skin removed

½ cup chicken broth

1 to 2 teaspoons butter

Combine the olive oil, soy sauce, vinegar, lemon juice, Worcestershire sauce, parsley, dry mustard, pepper and garlic in a bowl and mix well. Reserve 3 tablespoons of the marinade in a separate bowl. Combine the remaining marinade and the pork tenderloin in a large resealable plastic bag, turning to coat. Seal the bag and chill for 4 hours, turning occasionally.

Preheat the oven to 350 degrees.

Remove the tenderloin from the marinade, discarding the marinade. Bring the tenderloin to room temperature. Place in a hot ovenproof skillet and sear each side of the tenderloin over medium-high heat for 2 to 3 minutes. Place the skillet in the oven and cook for 30 to 40 minutes or until a meat thermometer inserted in the center of the tenderloin registers 160 degrees. Remove the tenderloin to a cutting board, reserving the drippings in the skillet. Let stand for 5 minutes before slicing.

Meanwhile, place the skillet over medium-high heat. Add the chicken broth and bring to a boil, scraping up any browned bits. Stir the reserved marinade and add to the skillet. Boil for 2 to 3 minutes, stirring frequently. Add the butter. Remove from the heat and stir until the butter is melted. Arrange the sliced tenderloin on a serving dish and pour the sauce evenly over the tenderloin.

Osso Buco

Perfect for the first cold Sunday of the season. Makes your house smell divine. Love to serve this with polenta or mashed potatoes.

1 cup unbleached all-purpose flour

Salt and freshly ground black pepper to taste

1 (12- to 14-pound) veal shank, cut into 16 (2-inch-thick) sections

½ cup olive oil

½ cup sweet butter

2 medium yellow onions, coarsely chopped

6 large garlic cloves, peeled and chopped

½ teaspoon dried basil

½ teaspoon dried oregano

1 (28-ounce) can Italian plum tomatoes, drained

2 cups dry white wine

2 cups beef stock

¾ cup chopped Italian parsley

Grated zest of 2 lemons

Combine the flour, salt and pepper in a shallow dish. Coat the veal with the flour mixture. Heat the olive oil and butter in a Dutch oven and sear the veal, browning well on all sides. Remove the veal to paper towels to drain, reserving the drippings.

Add the onions, garlic, basil and oregano to the drippings and cook for 10 minutes, stirring occasionally. Add the tomatoes and season with salt and pepper. Cook for 10 minutes longer. Skim off the excess fat.

Add the wine and bring to a boil. Reduce the heat and simmer, uncovered, for 15 minutes.

Preheat the oven to 350 degrees. Return the veal shanks to the Dutch oven and add just enough of the beef stock to cover. Bake, covered, for 1½ hours. Bake, uncovered, for 30 minutes or until the veal is very tender.

Sprinkle with the parsley and lemon zest and serve immediately.

Diane's Lamb Chops

Juice of 2 lemons
2 to 3 garlic cloves, finely chopped

Salt and pepper to taste
3 sprigs of rosemary, chopped
10 lamb chops, Frenched

Combine the lemon juice, garlic, salt, pepper and rosemary in a bowl and mix well. Marinate the lamb chops in the marinade in the refrigerator for 4 to 6 hours, turning once. Let stand at room temperature for 30 minutes before grilling. Grill on Medium-High for 3 minutes per side or until cooked to the desired degree of doneness. Serve with your favorite vegetables. Scalloped potatoes or lightly sautéed green beans and mushrooms with lemon vinaigrette make a good combination.

Chicken and Noodles with Peanut Sauce

5 ounces Japanese chuka soba noodles
½ cup fat-free reduced-sodium chicken broth
⅓ cup hoisin sauce
¼ cup creamy peanut butter
2 tablespoons rice vinegar
2 tablespoons ketchup
¼ teaspoon crushed red pepper

2 teaspoons dark sesame oil, divided
1 pound chicken breast tenders, cut into 1-inch pieces
1½ cups red bell pepper strips
1 tablespoon bottled minced ginger
1 teaspoon bottled minced garlic
½ cup chopped green onions, divided

Cook the noodles according to the package directions; drain. Combine the broth, hoisin sauce, peanut butter, vinegar, ketchup and crushed red pepper in a bowl; stir well using a whisk. Heat 1 teaspoon of the sesame oil in a large nonstick skillet over medium-high heat. Add the chicken and sauté for 4 minutes. Add the bell pepper and sauté for 3 minutes. Combine the chicken mixture and noodles in a large bowl. Cook the ginger and garlic for 15 seconds in the remaining sesame oil in a saucepan over medium heat. Stir in the broth mixture and cook for 30 seconds, stirring constantly. Add the broth mixture and ¼ cup green onions to the noodle mixture and toss well. Sprinkle with the remaining green onions.

Chicken Lasagne Bake

8 ounces lasagna

1 (10-ounce) can cream of chicken soup, undiluted

1 cup chicken broth

½ teaspoon salt

6 ounces cream cheese, softened

1 cup cottage cheese

½ cup sour cream

½ cup mayonnaise or salad dressing

⅓ cup chopped onion

⅓ cup chopped green bell pepper

⅓ cup chopped pimento-stuffed olives

¼ cup finely chopped fresh parsley

3 cups chopped cooked chicken or shredded rotisserie chicken

½ cup fine dry breadcrumbs

1 tablespoon butter, melted

Cook the noodles according to package directions; drain. Rinse with cold water; drain and set aside.

Preheat the oven to 375 degrees. Grease a 9x13-inch baking dish lightly.

Combine the soup, broth and salt in a large bowl and stir until smooth. Set aside.

Combine the cream cheese, cottage cheese, sour cream and mayonnaise in a large mixing bowl. Beat at medium speed for 1 minute or until smooth. Stir in the onion, bell pepper, olives and parsley. Set aside.

Layer half each of the noodles, cream cheese mixture, chicken and soup mixture in the prepared baking dish. Repeat the layers. Mix the breadcrumbs and butter and sprinkle over the top of the soup mixture.

Bake for 25 to 30 minutes or until hot and bubbly.

Chicken Osso Buco

8 medium chicken drumsticks or thighs

2 tablespoons all-purpose flour

2 tablespoons olive oil

½ cup chopped carrots

½ cup chopped onion

½ cup chopped celery

4 garlic cloves, minced

½ cup dry white wine or chicken broth

1 (8-ounce) can tomato sauce

¼ cup chicken broth

1 teaspoon finely shredded lemon peel

1 tablespoon lemon juice

1 sprig of thyme

1 bay leaf

2 cups penne

Snipped fresh parsley for garnish

Remove the skin from the chicken. Place the flour in a plastic bag. Add the chicken, a few pieces at a time, shaking to coat. Cook the chicken in the hot olive oil in a 10-inch skillet over medium heat for 5 minutes per side or until golden brown. Remove the chicken and set aside.

Add the carrots, onion, celery and garlic to the skillet. Sauté for 4 to 5 minutes or until lightly browned. Add the wine carefully to the skillet, scraping up any browned bits. Stir in the tomato sauce, broth, lemon peel, lemon juice, thyme and bay leaf.

Return the chicken to the skillet. Bring the mixture to a boil; reduce the heat. Simmer, covered, for 35 to 40 minutes longer or until the chicken is cooked through. Discard the thyme and bay leaf.

Meanwhile, cook the penne according to the package directions; drain well.

Spoon the chicken and sauce over the pasta in a serving dish. Garnish with parsley sprigs.

Chicken Potpie

1 (2½-pound) broiler-fryer chicken

2 quarts water

2 teaspoons salt, divided

5⅓ tablespoons butter

1 cup chopped onion

1 cup chopped celery

1 cup chopped carrots

1 small potato, peeled and chopped

½ cup frozen English peas, thawed

½ cup plus 1 teaspoon all-purpose flour, divided

1 cup half-and-half

½ teaspoon pepper

½ (15-ounce) package refrigerated piecrusts

Bring the chicken, water and 1 teaspoon of the salt to a boil in a Dutch oven. Reduce the heat to low and simmer, covered, for 1 hour. Remove the chicken from the broth. Chop the chicken, discarding the skin and bones. Set the chicken aside. Skim the fat from the broth, reserving 2 cups of the broth.

Preheat the oven to 400 degrees. Grease a 7x11-inch baking dish lightly.

Melt the butter in a large skillet. Add the onion, celery, carrots, potato and peas. Cook for 10 minutes or until the carrots are tender, stirring constantly. Add ½ cup of the flour, stirring until smooth. Gradually add the half-and-half and reserved broth. Cook over medium heat until the mixture is thick and bubbly, stirring constantly. Stir in the chopped chicken. Season with the remaining salt and pepper. Pour into the prepared baking dish and set aside.

Unfold the piecrust and press out the fold lines; sprinkle with the remaining flour, spreading over the surface of the crust.

Roll the pastry into an 8x12-inch rectangle and place over the filling. Fold the edges under and crimp. Cut slits in the top to allow steam to escape.

Bake for 30 minutes or until the crust is golden brown, covering the edges with foil after 20 minutes to prevent excessive browning.

Chicken Spaghetti

1½ green bell peppers, chopped

1 onion, chopped

1 cup butter

1 tablespoon chicken base

¼ cup all-purpose flour

1 quart milk

1 pound Velveeta cheese, cut into cubes

2 (10-ounce) cans cream of mushroom soup

1 (4-ounce) can sliced mushrooms

1 (4-ounce) jar pimentos

8 ounces spaghetti, cooked

1 pound chicken, cooked and cubed or shredded

Preheat the oven to 350 degrees.

Sauté the bell peppers and onion in the butter and chicken base in a skillet until tender. Add the flour and cook until the mixture is thickened, stirring constantly. Add the milk and stir until creamy. Add the cheese and cook until melted, stirring constantly.

Add the soup, mushrooms, pimentos, spaghetti and chicken to the sauce. Pour into a casserole dish and bake for 30 minutes.

Roasted Chicken with Lemon and Rosemary

2 garlic bulbs, minced

1 cup fresh lemon juice

1½ teaspoons pepper

1 tablespoon salt

⅔ cup chopped fresh rosemary

2 cups olive oil

3 chickens, cut up

3 lemons, sliced

Whisk the garlic, lemon juice, pepper, salt and rosemary in a bowl until blended. Whisk in the olive oil. Divide the mixture evenly among 3 large heavy-duty resealable plastic bags. Add the chickens and the lemons. Seal the bags and chill for 8 hours, turning the bags occasionally.

Preheat the oven to 425 degrees. Remove the chickens from the marinade and arrange in baking dishes. Drizzle with the remaining marinade.

Bake for 1 hour or until the chicken is cooked through, basting with the pan juices every 20 minutes.

Chicken Stroganoff

2 tablespoons olive oil, divided

3 medium yellow onions, thinly sliced into rings

1 green bell pepper, seeded and thinly sliced

8 ounces (15 medium) button mushrooms, thinly sliced

1½ teaspoons kosher salt, divided

½ teaspoon freshly ground black pepper, divided

4 boneless skinless chicken breast halves, cut into ½-inch-thick strips

1 cup dry white wine

1 cup reduced-sodium chicken broth

2 tablespoons barbecue sauce

1 teaspoon Worcestershire sauce

2 tablespoons Dijon mustard

1 teaspoon hot sauce

½ cup sour cream

Rice, pasta or toast

Heat 1 tablespoon of the olive oil in a large saucepan over medium heat. Add the onions and cook for 8 minutes or until tender, stirring frequently. Add the bell pepper, mushrooms, ½ teaspoon of the salt and ¼ teaspoon of the pepper. Cook for 6 minutes or until the mushrooms release liquid and are tender. Pour the vegetables into a colander, reserving the vegetables and ½ cup of the liquid.

Return the pan to the heat and add the remaining olive oil. Season the chicken with the remaining salt and pepper. Cook the chicken in batches for 5 minutes or until golden brown and cooked through. Add the chicken to the colander with the vegetables. Pour the wine, broth and reserved vegetable liquid into the pan and bring to a boil, scraping up any browned bits. Add the barbecue sauce, Worcestershire, mustard and hot sauce and whisk until smooth. Boil the liquid down to 1¼ cups or to half its original amount. The liquid should thicken slightly. Reduce the heat and whisk in the sour cream; do not let the sauce boil. Return the vegetables and chicken to the pan and simmer until heated through.

Serve over rice, pasta or toast.

Chicken Thighs, Red Onions and Balsamic Vinegar

The chicken is smothered in a thick onion sauce; serve over mashed potatoes.

- 2 teaspoons olive oil
- 1 pound (3 medium) red onions, cut into slices and separated into rings
- ½ teaspoon coarsely ground black pepper, divided
- ¼ teaspoon salt, divided
- 4 chicken thighs, skinned
- ¼ teaspoon dried oregano
- ¼ teaspoon dried marjoram
- 4 teaspoons balsamic vinegar, divided
- 2 tablespoons chopped fresh flat-leaf parsley

Heat the olive oil in a large nonstick skillet over medium heat. Add the onions, ¼ teaspoon of the pepper and ⅛ teaspoon of the salt and sauté for 5 minutes.

Add the remaining pepper, salt, chicken, oregano and marjoram to the skillet and sprinkle with 3 teaspoons of the vinegar. Reduce the heat to low and simmer, covered, for 25 minutes or until the chicken is cooked through. Increase the heat and cook, uncovered, for 2 minutes or until most of the liquid has evaporated. Stir in the remaining vinegar and sprinkle with the parsley. Serve with lemon wedges.

Curried Chicken with Dried Cranberries and Cherries

3 teaspoons canola oil, divided

2 pounds boneless skinless chicken breast halves, trimmed of fat and cut crosswise into ½-inch-thick slices, divided

3 tablespoons mild or medium-hot curry powder, divided

2 teaspoons butter

1 small onion, chopped

1 tablespoon yellow mustard seeds

¾ teaspoon ground cardamom or cloves

1 (15-ounce) can diced tomatoes and green chilies

1½ cups reduced-sodium chicken broth

1⅓ cups dried cranberries

1 cup dried cherries

1 tablespoon minced fresh ginger

¼ teaspoon salt, or to taste

Chopped cilantro for garnish

Heat 1½ teaspoons canola oil in a nonreactive Dutch oven over medium-high heat until hot but not smoking. Add half the chicken and sprinkle with ½ teaspoon of the curry powder. Cook for 5 minutes or until the chicken begins to brown, stirring occasionally. Remove to a large plate. Add the remaining canola oil to the pot and heat until hot. Add the remaining chicken and sprinkle with ½ teaspoon of the curry powder. Cook for 5 minutes or until the chicken begins to brown, stirring occasionally. Remove to the plate.

Add the butter, onion and mustard seeds to the pot. Cook for 2 to 4 minutes, stirring until the seeds pop and the onion begins to brown. Return the chicken and any accumulated juices to the pot. Sprinkle with the remaining curry powder and cardamom and stir to coat the chicken with the spices. Cook for 1 minute, stirring constantly.

Stir in the tomatoes, broth, cranberries, cherries, ginger and salt. Bring to a boil. Reduce the heat. Simmer, uncovered, for 10 to 12 minutes or until the mixture reduces slightly and the chicken is cooked through.

Garnish with cilantro. Serve with brown rice and your favorite green vegetable. Sautéed spinach goes well with this dish.

Healthy Chicken Enchiladas

Nonstick cooking spray

4 (4-ounce) boneless skinless chicken breasts

4 green onions

2 tablespoons chopped cilantro

1 jalapeño, seeded and minced

3 (10-ounce) cans green enchilada sauce, divided

8 corn tortillas

1 cup reduced-fat Cheddar cheese, shredded

2 cups shredded lettuce

½ cup salsa

½ cup light sour cream

1 tomato, diced

1 (2-ounce) can ripe olives, sliced

Preheat the oven to 350 degrees. Spray a 9x13-inch baking dish lightly with cooking spray.

Place the chicken in a large pot and add enough water to cover. Bring to a boil over high heat. Reduce the heat to medium and simmer for 15 minutes or until the chicken is cooked through; drain. Let stand to cool slightly. Shred the chicken using 2 forks; set aside.

Spray a large skillet lightly with cooking spray and sauté the green onions, cilantro and jalapeño for 2 minutes over medium-high heat. Add the shredded chicken and 1 can of the enchilada sauce. Cook for 5 minutes or until heated through, stirring occasionally.

Pour the remaining enchilada sauce into a medium bowl and microwave for 2 minutes or until warm. Dip each tortilla in the heated sauce and spoon an eighth of the chicken mixture onto the center. Roll up the tortillas to enclose the mixture and place seam side down in the prepared baking dish.

Pour the remaining heated sauce over the enchiladas and sprinkle with the cheese. Bake for 15 minutes or until the enchiladas are heated through and the cheese is melted.

Divide the lettuce among 4 plates and spoon a portion of the enchiladas on top. Add a spoonful of salsa and a dollop of sour cream. Sprinkle with tomato and olives.

Slow Cooker Chicken and Cornbread Dressing

CORNBREAD

- 1 egg, lightly beaten
- 2 cups buttermilk
- 2 cups self-rising yellow cornmeal mix
- ¼ teaspoon salt
- ½ cup butter, melted

CHICKEN AND DRESSING

- 1 rotisserie chicken, shredded
- 1 recipe cornbread, crumbled
- 8 slices of day-old bread, torn
- 2 ribs of celery, chopped
- 1 yellow onion, chopped
- 2 garlic cloves, chopped
- ¼ cup chopped fresh sage
- 2 tablespoons chopped fresh thyme
- 1 teaspoon kosher salt
- 1 teaspoon ground black pepper
- 4 eggs, lightly beaten
- 2 (14-ounce) cans chicken broth
- 2 (10-ounce) cans cream of chicken soup
- 1 (10-ounce) can cream of mushroom soup
- 3 tablespoons butter

For the Cornbread, preheat the oven to 450 degrees. Grease a 10-inch cast-iron skillet lightly and place in the oven to heat for 5 minutes.

Combine the egg and buttermilk in a large bowl and stir to mix well. Add the cornmeal and salt, stirring until the ingredients are mixed. Add the butter, stirring to mix. Pour the mixture into the prepared skillet. Bake for 15 to 20 minutes or until the cornbread is golden brown and begins to pull away from the sides of the pan. Let the bread cool in the skillet for 20 minutes. Remove to a wire rack to cool completely.

For the Chicken and Dressing, combine the chicken, cornbread, bread, celery, onion, garlic, sage, thyme, salt and pepper in a 4-quart slow cooker and mix well.

Whisk the eggs, broth, cream of chicken soup and cream of mushroom soup in a large bowl. Pour over the chicken mixture and mix well. Dot with the butter. Cook on High for 3 hours or on Low for 4 to 5 hours, stirring halfway through the cooking time.

NOTE: May mix 4 teaspoons baking powder and 1 teaspoon salt with 2 cups of cornmeal to make your own self-rising cornmeal.

Stuffed Chicken Breasts with Artichoke Hearts and Goat Cheese

2 teaspoons olive oil, divided

¾ cup chopped canned artichoke hearts

¼ cup minced shallots (about 3 shallots)

¼ cup (1-ounce) crumbled goat or feta cheese

1 teaspoon dried herbes de Provence or thyme, divided

¼ teaspoon salt, divided

¼ teaspoon black pepper, divided

4 (4-ounce) boneless skinless chicken breast halves

1 cup fat-free, less-sodium chicken broth

2 tablespoons fresh lemon juice

2 teaspoons cornstarch

Chopped fresh parsley for garnish

Lemon peel strips for garnish

Heat 1 teaspoon of the olive oil in a nonstick skillet over medium heat. Add the artichokes and shallots and sauté for 4 minutes. Transfer the vegetables to a bowl. Add the cheese, ½ teaspoon of the herbes de Provence, ⅛ teaspoon of the salt and ⅛ teaspoon of the pepper and mix well.

Cut a horizontal slit through the thickest portion of each breast to form a pocket. Stuff 2 tablespoons of the artichoke mixture into each pocket.

Heat the remaining olive oil in a large nonstick skillet over medium heat. Add the chicken and season with the remaining salt and pepper. Cook for 6 minutes per side or until cooked through. Transfer the chicken to a plate and keep warm. Add the broth and remaining herbes de Provence to the skillet and bring to a boil. Mix the lemon juice and cornstarch in a bowl. Add to the broth mixture, stirring with a whisk. Cook for 1 minute or until thick. Return the chicken to the pan. Cook, covered, for 2 minutes or until thoroughly heated. Garnish with parsley and lemon strips.

Turkey Chile Relleno Casserole

½ pound ground turkey

1 cup chopped onion

1¾ teaspoons ground cumin

1½ teaspoons dried oregano

½ teaspoon garlic powder

½ teaspoon salt

¼ teaspoon black pepper

1 (16-ounce) can fat-free refried beans

2 (4-ounce) cans whole green chilies, drained and cut lengthwise into quarters, divided

1 cup shredded Colby Jack cheese, divided

1 cup frozen whole kernel corn, thawed and drained

⅓ cup all-purpose flour

Salt to taste

1⅓ cups skim milk

⅛ teaspoon hot sauce

2 large eggs, lightly beaten

2 large egg whites, lightly beaten

Red onion slices for garnish

Chopped cilantro for garnish

Preheat the oven to 350 degrees.

Cook the ground turkey with the onion in a nonstick skillet over medium heat until browned, stirring to crumble. Remove from the heat and add the cumin, oregano, garlic, ½ teaspoon salt, pepper and beans. Stir well and set aside.

Arrange half of the green chilies in a 7x11-inch baking dish. Sprinkle with ½ cup of the cheese. Spoon mounds of the turkey mixture onto the cheese and spread gently, leaving a ¼-inch border around the edge of the dish. Add the corn in an even layer. Arrange the remaining green chilies over the corn and top with the remaining cheese.

Combine the flour and salt to taste in a bowl. Gradually add the milk, hot sauce, eggs and egg whites, stirring with a whisk until blended. Pour over the casserole. Bake for 1 hour and 5 minutes or until set. Let stand for 5 minutes. Garnish with onion slices and cilantro.

NOTE: Two small cans of chopped green chilies can be substituted for the whole chilies.

Prawns Stuffed with Goat Cheese on Tomato Coulis

TOMATO COULIS

- 1 tablespoon olive oil
- 4 large tomatoes, peeled, seeded and coarsely chopped
- 2 tablespoons minced cilantro
- 1 tablespoon minced seeded jalapeño or serrano pepper
- Juice of 1 lime
- Salt and pepper to taste

PRAWNS

- 1 pound large prawns or shrimp
- ¼ pound goat cheese
- ¼ pound natural cream cheese
- 1 garlic clove, peeled and minced
- 2 tablespoons minced cilantro
- 2 teaspoons heavy cream
- Salt and pepper to taste

For the Tomato Coulis, heat the olive oil in a sauté pan or skillet over medium heat. Add the tomatoes and cook, covered, for 5 minutes. Add the cilantro and jalapeño. Increase the heat to medium-high and cook, uncovered, until all the moisture has evaporated, stirring frequently. Add the lime juice, salt and pepper. Keep the coulis warm while preparing the prawns.

For the Prawns, preheat the oven to 350 degrees.

Remove the shells from the prawns, leaving the tails intact. Devein the prawns and then butterfly them by slicing down the curve but not cutting all the way through. Flatten slightly.

Mix the goat cheese, cream cheese, garlic, cilantro, cream, salt and pepper in a bowl and set aside.

Bake the prawns on a baking sheet for 3 minutes. Remove from the oven. Increase the oven temperature to 400 degrees. Pipe the cheese mixture onto the backs of the prawns using a pastry bag or a plastic bag with a hole cut in one corner. Bake for 3 minutes longer. Serve with the Tomato Coulis.

Linguine with Shrimp Scampi

Olive oil for pasta

2 tablespoons salt, divided

1½ pounds linguine

6 tablespoons unsalted butter

5 tablespoons olive oil

9 garlic cloves, minced (about 3 tablespoons),

2 pounds large shrimp (about 32 shrimp), peeled and deveined

½ teaspoon freshly ground black pepper

¾ cup chopped fresh parsley

Lemon zest to taste

½ cup fresh lemon juice (about 4 lemons)

½ lemon, cut into thinly sliced half rounds

¼ teaspoon hot red pepper flakes

Drizzle some olive oil in a large pot of boiling water. Add 1 tablespoon of salt and the linguine. Cook for 7 to 10 minutes or according to the package directions.

Meanwhile, heat the butter and 5 tablespoons olive oil in a large heavy saucepan over medium-low heat. Add the garlic and sauté for 1 minute, watching carefully so the garlic doesn't burn. Add the shrimp, remaining salt and pepper. Sauté for 5 minutes or just until the shrimp have turned pink, stirring frequently. Remove from the heat. Add the parsley, lemon zest, lemon juice, lemon slices and red pepper flakes and toss to mix.

Drain the cooked linguine and then return to the pot. Add the shrimp and sauce and toss to mix. Serve immediately.

Lisa's Mediterranean Shrimp

This is Debbie's sister's recipe and is often requested by the Watts clan!

1 cup (about 5 ounces) whole wheat orzo

Vegetable or canola oil for pasta

1½ tablespoons vegetable or canola oil

2 medium garlic cloves, minced (about 2 teaspoons garlic)

½ teaspoon red chili flakes (optional)

2 cups 2-inch asparagus pieces

Salt and pepper

1½ pounds peeled and deveined fresh medium shrimp

½ cup chopped fresh basil leaves, divided

4 tablespoons fresh lemon juice (about 2 lemons)

1 tablespoon extra-virgin olive oil

½ cup crumbled Mediterranean or regular feta cheese

Bring salted water to a boil in a large pot over high heat. Add the orzo and cook according to package directions until al dente; drain. Transfer to a bowl and toss with a small amount of vegetable oil.

Heat 1½ tablespoons vegetable oil in a large skillet over medium heat until the oil is shimmery. Add the garlic and chili flakes. Cook for 1 minute or until the mixture is fragrant but not browned, stirring constantly. Add the asparagus, salt and pepper and stir to coat the asparagus with oil. Cook for 3 to 4 minutes or until the asparagus is crisp-tender. Push the asparagus to the side of the pan. Add the shrimp and cook for 4 minutes or until pink and opaque, turning occasionally.

Add the orzo, most of the basil, lemon juice, olive oil and cheese to the pan, stirring to mix. Allow the orzo to heat through and adjust the seasonings to taste. Sprinkle with the remaining basil. Serve immediately.

Shrimp and Crab Gumbo

Our first book has a wonderful gumbo recipe; this recipe is another option.

⅓ cup all-purpose flour

3 slices of bacon, diced

2 cups finely chopped onion

1½ cups finely chopped green bell pepper (about 1 large)

4 ribs of celery, thinly sliced

4 garlic cloves, minced

1 cup water

2 (14-ounce) cans fat-free, less-sodium chicken broth, divided

2 teaspoons salt-free Cajun seasoning

½ teaspoon salt

¼ teaspoon crushed red pepper

1 (16-ounce) package frozen cut okra, thawed

1 pound medium shrimp, peeled and deveined

2 (6-ounce) cans lump crabmeat, drained

3 cups cooked long-grain white rice

Place the flour in a small skillet. Cook for 5 minutes over medium heat or until the flour is brown, stirring constantly. Place in a small bowl to cool.

Cook the bacon in a Dutch oven over medium-high heat for 3 minutes. Add the onion, bell pepper, celery and garlic. Sauté for 10 minutes or until the vegetables are tender and lightly browned. Add the water and cook for 1 minute, stirring constantly.

Combine the toasted flour and 1 can of the broth in a medium bowl, stirring well with a whisk. Pour the broth mixture gradually into the pan with the vegetables. Stir in the remaining broth, Cajun seasoning, salt, crushed red pepper and okra. Bring to a boil. Reduce the heat and simmer, covered, for 15 minutes.

Add the shrimp and cook for 3 minutes or until the shrimp are done. Stir in the crabmeat gently. Remove from the heat and serve the gumbo over the rice while it is still hot. Serve with hot pepper sauce.

Shrimp and Orzo with Cherry Tomatoes and Romano Cheese

1 cup uncooked orzo

2 tablespoons olive oil, divided

1 pound medium shrimp, peeled and deveined

¾ teaspoon salt, divided

¼ teaspoon black pepper, divided

1 cup chopped sweet onion

1 tablespoon minced garlic

¼ teaspoon crushed red pepper

2 cups halved cherry tomatoes

⅓ cup grated fresh pecorino Romano cheese

⅓ cup chopped fresh basil

Cook the pasta according to the package directions, omitting the salt and fat; drain well.

Meanwhile, heat 1 tablespoon of the olive oil in a large skillet over medium-high heat. Add the shrimp and sprinkle ½ teaspoon salt and ⅛ teaspoon pepper evenly over the shrimp. Cook the shrimp for 1½ minutes per side or until done. Transfer the shrimp to a plate.

Add the remaining olive oil to the skillet. Add the onion, garlic and red pepper and cook for 2 minutes, stirring frequently. Add the tomatoes and cook for 3 minutes or until the tomatoes begin to soften, stirring occasionally. Stir in the pasta and shrimp and cook for 1 minute or until thoroughly heated. Remove from the heat and stir in the remaining salt, pepper, cheese and basil.

Southern Smothered Shrimp

2 slices of bacon

1 tablespoon unsalted butter

½ medium onion, chopped

1 rib of celery, chopped

1 garlic clove, minced

1 tablespoon all-purpose flour

2 cups chopped plum tomatoes

1 cup chicken broth

1 pound (15 to 20) large shrimp, peeled and deveined

Salt and pepper to taste

¼ teaspoon chopped fresh thyme

Juice from ½ lemon

Chopped fresh parsley to taste

2 cups cooked white rice

Cook the bacon in a skillet over medium heat for 5 minutes or until crisp and brown. Transfer the bacon to a paper towel and set aside.

Add the butter to the skillet. Add the onion, celery and garlic and cook for 6 minutes or until the onion is translucent, stirring frequently. Sprinkle with the flour and mix well. Add the tomatoes and broth. Crumble the bacon and add to the tomato mixture. Bring to a boil over high heat.

Reduce the heat to medium-low and simmer, partially covered, for 25 minutes or until the mixture is thickened.

Stir in the shrimp and increase the heat to high. Cook for 3 to 5 minutes or until the shrimp are firm, stirring frequently.

Season with salt, pepper, thyme and lemon juice. Sprinkle with the parsley and serve over rice.

Salmon Cakes

RÉMOULADE SAUCE

¾ cup mayonnaise

2 teaspoons Dijon mustard

1½ teaspoons yellow mustard

1 teaspoon dried tarragon

¼ teaspoon hot sauce

2 teaspoons tiny capers, drained and chopped

1 tablespoon chopped flat-leaf parsley

1 scallion, very thinly sliced

CAKES

2 (7-ounce) cans pink salmon

½ cup finely diced onion

½ cup finely diced celery

½ teaspoon dried tarragon

Salt and pepper to taste

½ cup mayonnaise

1 tablespoon Dijon mustard

1 egg, lightly beaten

1⅓ cups crushed cracker crumbs, divided

8 medium carrots, peeled

1 tablespoon corn oil

1 tablespoon unsalted butter

For the Rémoulade Sauce, combine the mayonnaise, Dijon mustard, yellow mustard, tarragon, hot sauce, capers, parsley and scallion in a small bowl and mix well. Set aside, covered, in the refrigerator.

For the Cakes, drain the salmon well in a strainer; do not squeeze.

Flake the salmon carefully into a bowl, discarding any small bones, cartilage and skin. Add the onion, celery, tarragon, salt and pepper and fold together using a rubber spatula.

Combine the mayonnaise and mustard in a small bowl and mix well. Fold into the salmon mixture. Fold in the egg and ⅓ cup of the cracker crumbs.

Shape the mixture into 8 patties and coat with the remaining cracker crumbs. Refrigerate, loosely covered, for 1 hour.

Meanwhile, coarsely grate the carrots into a large bowl. Toss with ⅓ cup of the Rémoulade Sauce, using a fork to break up the clumps.

Heat the corn oil and butter in a nonstick skillet. Add the cakes and cook over medium heat for 3 to 4 minutes per side or until the cakes are golden brown, adding additional corn oil and butter if necessary.

Serve the cakes topped with a dollop of Rémoulade Sauce and with the carrots alongside.

Salmon in Parchment

8 ounces thin spaghetti

1 tablespoon olive oil

¼ teaspoon salt

2 tablespoons chopped fresh dill
or parsley

1 (24-ounce) salmon fillet, cut
into four 6-ounce pieces

2 tablespoons Dijon mustard

4 large sheets of parchment
paper

1 cup julienned carrots

1 cup julienned zucchini

1 cup asparagus tips

1 cup julienned red bell pepper

Preheat the oven to 400 degrees.

Cook the spaghetti in a pan of rapidly boiling water until al dente. Drain the
spaghetti and toss with the olive oil, salt and dill.

Rinse the salmon fillets. Pat dry and place on a plate. Spread ½ tablespoon of
the mustard evenly over the top of each fillet.

Place a fourth of the pasta on the center of each sheet of parchment
paper. Top with a salmon fillet and add ¼ cup each of the carrots, zucchini,
asparagus and bell pepper. Fold the parchment paper around each fillet,
securing tightly.

Place the pouches on a baking sheet. Bake on the middle rack for 10 minutes.
Serve immediately in the sealed pouches, allowing guests to open the
pouches just before eating.

Crisp Tilapia

Excellent tilapia dish.

4 (6- to 8-ounce) tilapia fillets

1 cup heavy cream, divided

1 cup yellow cornmeal

1½ teaspoons salt, divided

1 (1-ounce) envelope guacamole mix

2 tablespoons vegetable oil, divided

1 (7-ounce) can picante salsa verde

1 cup creamed corn

Place the tilapia in a shallow dish and cover with ½ cup of the heavy cream; set aside.

Combine the cornmeal, ½ teaspoon salt and guacamole mix in a shallow bowl and mix well.

Heat a nonstick skillet over medium-high heat for 2 minutes. Remove the tilapia fillets from the cream and shake off the excess cream. Add 1 tablespoon of the vegetable oil to the skillet. Press each tilapia fillet into the cornmeal mixture and coat evenly. Place 2 tilapia fillets in the skillet and cook for 4 minutes; turn and cook for 4 minutes longer. Remove the fillets from the skillet and keep warm. Cook the remaining two fillets in the remaining vegetable oil.

Combine the salsa verde, corn and remaining cream in a saucepan and bring to a boil. Reduce the heat and simmer for 5 minutes or until slightly thickened. Season with the remaining salt. Serve with the tilapia.

Fettuccine with Prosciutto and Asparagus

3 cups diagonally cut 1-inch asparagus pieces

9 ounces fresh fettuccine

1 tablespoon olive oil

1 cup chopped onion

2 teaspoons bottled minced garlic

½ cup chopped prosciutto (about 2 ounces)

2 teaspoons balsamic vinegar

½ teaspoon salt

⅛ teaspoon crushed red pepper

⅛ teaspoon black pepper

¼ cup shredded fresh Parmesan cheese

Cook the asparagus and pasta in a pot of boiling water for 5 minutes or until the pasta is al dente. Drain the asparagus and pasta in a colander over a bowl, reserving ½ cup of the cooking liquid.

Wipe the pot dry using a paper towel. Heat the olive oil in the pot over medium heat. Sauté the onion and garlic in the oil for 2 minutes, stirring frequently. Add the prosciutto and cook for 2 minutes, stirring frequently. Stir in the asparagus and pasta, reserved cooking liquid, vinegar, salt, red pepper and black pepper and toss well. Sprinkle with the Parmesan cheese.

Serve with a tossed garden salad or sliced tomatoes sprinkled with basil and feta cheese.

If you really want to make a friend, go to someone's house and eat with him . . . . the people who give you their food give you their heart.

CESAR CHAVEZ

Vail, Colorado

DINNER IN A SNAP

After a long and demanding day, it's sometimes nice to settle down and indulge in a satisfying home-cooked meal that comes together with very little fuss. We are pleased to offer a collection of delicious easy-to-cook dinner recipes that take full advantage of snappy marinades, quick combinations of pasta and sauce, and the miracle-making of crockpot, oven, and grill for impressive entertaining in a fast-paced, often exhausting world.

An Earl Family Favorite Dinner

2 (6- to 8-ounce) beef fillets

Urban Accents Mesa Rosa Chipotle Southwestern Smoky Blend seasoning

Let the beef stand at room temperature for 1 hour before cooking.

Preheat the oven to 350 degrees. Coat the beef on all sides with the seasoning. Heat a cast-iron skillet over high heat until very hot. Sear the beef for 4 to 5 minutes per side. Place in the oven and bake to the desired degree of doneness. Let the beef stand for 10 minutes before cutting.

Serve with brown rice and guacamole. A perfect combination!

NOTE: If you cannot find Urban Accents seasoning at your local grocery, it's well worth ordering from www.urbanaccents.com. We put it on shrimp, in our guacamole, etc. Very useful.

Mom's Meatloaf

Just like dressing, everyone's mom makes it best. Well, this is Diane's mom's recipe. She cannot visit her without having it.

2 (8-ounce) cans tomato sauce

½ onion, finely chopped

1 egg, well beaten

½ teaspoon salt

1 teaspoon pepper

12 saltine crackers, crushed

1 pound lean ground beef

Preheat the oven to 350 degrees.

Combine the tomato sauce, onion, egg, salt, pepper, crackers and ground beef in a bowl and mix thoroughly. Shape into a loaf and place in a loaf pan. Bake for 1 hour.

Bolognese Sauce

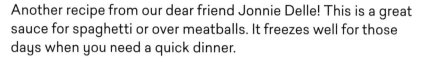

Another recipe from our dear friend Jonnie Delle! This is a great sauce for spaghetti or over meatballs. It freezes well for those days when you need a quick dinner.

2 pounds ground beef
1 medium onion, chopped
1 garlic clove, mashed
1 (6-ounce) can tomato paste
1 cup beef broth
½ cup red wine

½ cup water
1 tablespoon dried oregano
1 tablespoon dried basil
Pepper to taste
2 tablespoons heavy cream

Brown the ground beef with the onion and garlic in a medium saucepan over medium heat, stirring to crumble; drain. Stir in the tomato paste, broth, wine, water, oregano, basil and pepper. Bring to a boil. Reduce the heat and simmer for about 30 minutes. Stir in the cream. Serve with pasta of choice.

You don't need a silver fork to eat good food.
PAUL PRUDHOMME

Slow-Cooked Stroganoff

½ cup all-purpose flour

2 teaspoons salt

½ teaspoon pepper

1 teaspoon dried parsley

½ teaspoon dry mustard

3 pounds boneless beef, cut into pieces or strips, or cubed sirloin

1 large onion, chopped

2 (4-ounce) cans mushrooms, drained

1 (10-ounce) can concentrated beef broth

¼ cup red wine (optional)

1½ cups sour cream

Hot buttered noodles

Combine the flour, salt, pepper, parsley and dry mustard in a bowl and mix well. Add the beef and coat thoroughly with the flour mixture.

Layer the onion, mushrooms and beef in a 5-quart slow cooker. Pour the broth and wine over the beef. Cook, covered, for 6 to 7 hours or until the beef is the desired tenderness. Stir in the sour cream just before serving over the noodles.

The only real stumbling block is fear of failure. In cooking, you've got to have a what-the-hell attitude.

JULIA CHILD

Flank Steak in Mexican Marinade

1 (6-ounce) can pineapple juice

½ cup reduced-sodium soy sauce

¼ cup fresh lime juice

1 tablespoon ground cumin

1 teaspoon garlic salt

1 (1¾-pound) flank steak

Combine the pineapple juice, soy sauce, lime juice, cumin and garlic salt in a bowl and mix well. Reserve ¼ cup of the marinade in a small bowl in the refrigerator.

Place the steak in a large shallow dish or resealable plastic bag. Pour the remaining marinade over the steak. Chill, covered or sealed, for 3 to 4 hours, turning occasionally.

Preheat the grill to Medium-High (350 to 400 degrees). Remove the steak from the marinade. Grill, covered, for 15 minutes or until a meat thermometer inserted into the thickest portion of the steak registers 145 degrees for medium-rare, turning occasionally and basting with the reserved marinade.

Slice the steak and serve with tortillas, tomato, lettuce, guacamole, shredded cheese and sour cream.

Pork Scaloppine

1 tablespoon unsalted butter

1 tablespoon olive oil

6 to 8 tenderized thinly sliced pork cutlets

¼ teaspoon freshly ground black pepper

3 teaspoons kosher salt, divided

1 cup chicken broth

1 teaspoon lemon juice

Hot cooked noodles or rice

1 teaspoon lemon zest

Heat the butter and olive oil in a large nonstick skillet over medium heat. Season the pork cutlets with the pepper and 2 teaspoons of the salt. Cook in the hot butter mixture for 1 minute per side or until lightly browned and cooked through. Remove the cutlets to a plate and set aside.

Add the broth to the skillet and simmer for 5 minutes or until slightly thickened, scraping up any browned bits using a wooden spoon. Remove from the heat. Stir in the lemon juice and remaining salt. Place the noodles and pork cutlets in a serving dish. Drizzle with the sauce and sprinkle with the lemon zest.

Fiesta Pork Chops with Couscous

4 (¾-inch-thick) rib pork chops

Salt and pepper to taste

2 tablespoons vegetable oil

1 (8-ounce) can tomato sauce

1 cup chunky salsa

1 cup frozen whole kernel corn

¼ cup lemon or lime juice

2 cups hot cooked couscous

1 tablespoon cold water

1 teaspoon cornstarch

Chopped cilantro or parsley for garnish

Season both sides of the pork chops with salt and pepper. Cook in the vegetable oil in a large skillet over medium-high heat for 4 minutes or until brown, turning once. Drain off the oil and add the tomato sauce, salsa, corn and lemon juice. Bring to a boil. Reduce the heat. Simmer, covered, for 6 to 8 minutes or until the pork chops are no longer pink and the juices run clear. Place the couscous in a large serving dish. Remove the pork chops from the sauce to the serving dish; keep warm.

Combine the water and cornstarch in a small bowl and mix well. Add to the sauce and cook until thickened and bubbly, stirring frequently. Cook for 2 minutes longer, stirring frequently. Remove from the heat and spoon over the pork chops and couscous. Garnish with cilantro.

Pecan-Crusted Pork Tenderloin

Marinate a day ahead!

- ¼ cup apple cider
- 1 pound pork tenderloin, trimmed, or 4 butterflied pork chops
- Nonstick cooking spray
- ¼ cup packed brown sugar
- 1 tablespoon spicy brown mustard
- ½ teaspoon salt
- ¼ teaspoon pepper
- 2 garlic cloves, minced
- ⅔ cup chopped pecans

Combine the apple cider and pork in a resealable plastic bag. Seal and marinate in the refrigerator for 8 hours.

Preheat the oven to 400 degrees. Spray a broiler pan rack with nonstick cooking spray.

Remove the pork from the bag to a large plate, discarding the apple cider. Combine the brown sugar, mustard, salt, pepper and garlic in a bowl and mix well. Rub the mixture over the pork. Roll the pork in the pecans. Place the pork on the prepared rack in the broiler pan. Bake for 25 minutes or until a meat thermometer registers 160 degrees. Let stand for 10 minutes before serving.

Pulled Pork in a Crock Pot

A McKee favorite.

1 (5- to 7-pound) whole pork shoulder

Barbecue seasoning rub (Stubb's is good)

1 medium or large onion, cut into chunks

2 or 3 garlic cloves

Few pinches of kosher salt

Freshly ground black pepper to taste

1 to 2 tablespoons liquid smoke

Barbecue sauce

Buns

Packaged coleslaw

Coat the pork thoroughly with the seasoning rub. Place in a slow cooker. Add the onion, garlic, salt and pepper. Add the liquid smoke. Fill the slow cooker about two-thirds full with water. Cook on Low for 8 hours.

Remove the pork to a large bowl, discarding the cooking liquid. Shred the pork using two forks, discarding any fat or bones. Add the desired amount of barbecue sauce and mix well. Serve on buns with coleslaw on top of pork.

Chicken Skewers

⅓ cup hot water

¼ cup teriyaki marinade and sauce

¼ cup creamy peanut butter

¼ cup soy sauce

¼ cup chopped cilantro

2 tablespoons honey Dijon mustard

1 pound boneless skinless chicken breast halves, cut into 12 thin strips

Whisk the water, marinade, peanut butter, soy sauce, cilantro and mustard in a medium bowl. Add the chicken and marinate in the refrigerator for 1 to 2 hours.

Preheat the grill.

Skewer the chicken strips and grill until cooked through, turning occasionally.

Balsamic Chicken with Prosciutto

6 boneless skinless chicken breast halves, lightly pounded

3 tablespoons chopped sage

Salt and pepper to taste

1 cup all-purpose flour

3 tablespoons (about) extra-virgin olive oil

1½ cups unsalted chicken stock

2 ounces prosciutto, julienned

2 to 3 teaspoons balsamic vinegar

Sprinkle the chicken evenly with the sage and season lightly with the salt and pepper. Coat with the flour, shaking off any excess. Cook in batches in the olive oil in a large sauté pan over medium heat for 5 minutes per side or until golden brown. Remove to a platter. Add the stock to the pan gradually, whisking constantly. Add the prosciutto and vinegar. Bring to a boil. Reduce the heat to low and return the chicken to the pan. Cook for 7 to 10 minutes or until the juices run clear when the chicken is pierced with a knife, basting occasionally with the sauce. Transfer the chicken to a warm platter. Season the sauce with salt and pepper and serve with the chicken.

Chicken Piccata

This is Jan's daughter, Maura's, favorite home-from-college dinner.

4 boneless skinless chicken breast halves

¼ cup all-purpose flour

1 tablespoon each butter and olive oil

½ cup white wine

¼ cup fresh lemon juice

2 tablespoons capers

2 teaspoons minced fresh garlic

¼ teaspoon each salt and freshly ground pepper

8 ounces linguine, cooked

2 tablespoons chopped fresh flat-leaf parsley

Place each chicken breast between 2 sheets of plastic wrap and pound to ½-inch thickness using a meat mallet. Place the flour in a shallow dish and coat the chicken with the flour. Heat the butter and olive oil in a large skillet over medium-high heat. Add the chicken and cook for 3 minutes per side or until browned. Remove the chicken from the skillet; keep warm. Add the wine, lemon juice, capers and garlic to the skillet and scrape up any browned bits. Cook for 2 minutes or until thickened. Season with the salt and pepper. Serve the chicken over the pasta. Top with the sauce and sprinkle with the parsley.

Danny's Margherita Pasta

Very quick and easy but delicious!

8 ounces boneless skinless chicken breasts

8 ounces Italian sausage

8 ounces penne pasta

1 tablespoon minced garlic

2 tablespoons extra-virgin olive oil

1 tablespoon butter

1 pint cherry tomatoes, cut into halves

3 tablespoons shredded fresh Parmesan cheese

3 tablespoons chopped fresh basil

Preheat the oven to 350 degrees. Bake the chicken and the sausage in a baking pan for about 20 minutes or until the chicken is cooked through. Cut into bite-size pieces and set aside. Bring a pot of salted water to a boil. Add the pasta and cook for 9 minutes or until al dente; drain.

Meanwhile, sauté the garlic in the olive oil and butter in a skillet over medium heat for 1 or 2 minutes. Add the tomatoes and sauté briefly. Add the pasta, chicken and sausage. Add the Parmesan cheese and basil and cook until heated through, stirring frequently. Serve immediately with a fresh salad and crusty bread.

Faye's Chicken and Rice

This recipe is from Diane's precious mother-in-law. Perfect when you are in a comfort food mood!

½ cup butter

4 boneless skinless chicken breast halves, cooked and chopped

1 can cream of celery soup

1 can cream of chicken soup

1 can chicken broth

½ green bell pepper, chopped

1 small onion, chopped

1 jar pimento

1½ cups uncooked instant rice

Salt and pepper to taste

Preheat the oven to 350 degrees. Melt the butter in a large casserole dish. Arrange the chicken in the dish with the butter. Mix the cream of celery soup, cream of chicken soup, broth, bell pepper, onion, pimento, rice, salt and pepper in a large bowl and spoon over the chicken. Bake for 30 minutes.

Island Marinated Chicken

½ cup chopped onion

2 tablespoons vegetable oil

2 tablespoons brown sugar

¼ cup ketchup

1 tablespoon lime juice

½ teaspoon salt

½ teaspoon ground allspice

½ teaspoon ground ginger

¼ teaspoon onion powder

¼ teaspoon garlic powder

¼ teaspoon cayenne pepper

4 bone-in skinless chicken breasts

Preheat the grill.

Sauté the onion in the vegetable oil in a skillet until golden brown. Add the brown sugar, ketchup, lime juice, salt, allspice, ginger, onion powder, garlic powder and cayenne pepper and mix well. Boil the marinade for 1 minute. Reserve ¼ cup of the marinade. Marinate the chicken in the remaining marinade for 30 minutes. Grill until cooked through, turning and basting with the reserved marinade occasionally.

Jaron's Chicken Pasta

Stephanie's son's favorite

4 tablespoons butter

1 envelope Italian-style salad dressing mix

½ cup white wine

1 (10-ounce) can condensed golden mushroom soup

4 ounces cream cheese with chives

3 boneless skinless chicken breast halves

1 pound angel hair pasta

Preheat the oven to 325 degrees.

Melt the butter in a large saucepan over low heat. Stir in the dressing mix. Blend in the wine and soup. Add the cream cheese and cook until heated through and smooth, stirring constantly; do not boil. Arrange the chicken in a single layer in a 9x13-inch baking dish. Pour the sauce over the chicken. Bake for 1 hour.

Cook the pasta in boiling water for 5 minutes or until al dente; drain. Serve the chicken and sauce over the pasta.

Lemon Chicken and Rice with Artichokes

4 boneless chicken breasts, cut into small pieces

2¼ cups chopped onions

1 cup chopped red bell pepper

Nonstick cooking spray

2 cups uncooked instant rice

¼ cup fresh lemon juice

¼ teaspoon salt

¼ teaspoon black pepper

1 (14-ounce) can fat free, less-sodium chicken broth

1 (14-ounce) can quartered artichoke hearts, drained

2 tablespoons grated Romano cheese

Sauté the chicken, onions and bell pepper for 5 minutes in a Dutch oven coated with cooking spray over medium-high heat. Stir in the rice, lemon juice, salt, pepper and broth and bring to a boil. Reduce the heat and simmer, covered, for 15 minutes or until the rice is tender and the chicken is cooked through. Stir in the artichokes and cook for 1 minute or until heated through. Sprinkle with the Romano cheese.

Pecan Chicken Roll-Ups

4 boneless skinless chicken breasts

Fresh spinach leaves

1 cup chopped pecans

1 cup grated Parmesan cheese

¼ cup sherry

1 cup sour cream

1 (10-ounce) can cream of chicken soup

Preheat the oven to 350 degrees.

Pound the chicken breasts flat. Top each with a few leaves of spinach. Sprinkle each with ¼ cup of the pecans and 2 tablespoons of the Parmesan cheese. Roll up the chicken breasts and secure with wooden picks. Place the roll-ups in a shallow baking dish.

Combine the sherry, sour cream and soup in a bowl and mix well. Pour over the roll-ups and sprinkle with the remaining Parmesan cheese. Bake for 55 minutes.

Southwest Chicken and Spinach Casserole

3 medium yellow squash, thinly sliced

1 large red bell pepper, cut into ½-inch pieces

1 yellow onion, diced

2 tablespoons vegetable oil

1 (10-ounce) package frozen chopped spinach, thawed and drained

3 cups shredded cooked chicken or turkey

12 corn tortillas, cut into 1-inch strips

1 (10-ounce) can cream of celery soup

8 ounces sour cream

1 (8-ounce) jar picante sauce

1 can chopped green chilies, undrained

1 (1-ounce) envelope fajita seasoning

2 cups shredded Cheddar cheese, divided

Preheat the oven to 350 degrees. Grease a 9x13-inch baking dish lightly.

Sauté the squash, bell pepper and onion in the vegetable oil in a skillet for 6 minutes. Stir in the spinach.

Mix the squash mixture, chicken, tortillas, soup, sour cream, picante sauce, chilies, seasoning and 1½ cups of the cheese in a bowl and pour into the prepared baking dish. Bake, covered, for 30 minutes. Sprinkle with the remaining cheese and bake, uncovered, until the cheese is melted.

Cilantro Lime Shrimp
with Green Beans

Easy, easy!!

6 cups fresh green beans

6 garlic cloves, crushed, divided

  Salt and pepper to taste

1 cup water

2 teaspoons olive oil

2 pounds shrimp, shelled and deveined

1 lime

⅓ cup chopped fresh cilantro

Combine the green beans and 3 of the garlic cloves in a skillet. Season with salt and pepper. Cook over medium-high heat for 2 minutes, tossing frequently. Add the water and cook, covered, for 8 minutes longer. Cook, uncovered, until the water evaporates.

Meanwhile, heat a large frying pan over medium-high heat. Heat the olive oil in the pan and add the shrimp. Season with salt and pepper. Cook for 2 minutes. Turn over the shrimp and add the remaining 3 cloves of garlic. Sauté for 1 or 2 minutes or until the shrimp is cooked through, being careful not to overcook. Squeeze the juice of the lime over the shrimp and toss with the cilantro. Serve hot with the green beans.

Spicy Thai Coconut Shrimp

You just can't beat a good coconut shrimp!

2 cups uncooked rice

1½ tablespoons water

1½ teaspoons red curry paste or chile paste with garlic

1½ pounds medium shrimp, peeled and deveined

Nonstick cooking spray

2½ cups 1-inch asparagus pieces

1½ cups sliced green onions

½ teaspoon salt

1 (14-ounce) can light coconut milk

Cook the rice according to package directions, omitting the salt and fat.

Meanwhile, combine the water and curry paste in a medium bowl. Add the shrimp and toss to coat.

Heat a large nonstick skillet sprayed with cooking spray over medium-high heat until hot. Add the shrimp mixture and sauté for 4 minutes. Add the asparagus and green onions. Cook, covered, for 3 minutes or until the asparagus is crisp-tender.

Stir in the salt and coconut milk. Cook for 3 minutes or until heated through, stirring occasionally. Serve over the rice.

Hot 'n' Sweet Salmon

4 (4- to 6-ounce) salmon steaks
  or fillets

½ lime

1½ tablespoons ground red
  chili powder

1 tablespoon brown sugar

½ teaspoon salt

½ teaspoon paprika

¼ teaspoon cumin seeds

¼ teaspoon oregano flakes

¼ teaspoon cayenne pepper

Pat the salmon dry with paper towels and place on a plate. Squeeze the juice of the lime over the cut sides of the salmon.

Mix the chili powder, brown sugar, salt, paprika, cumin, oregano and cayenne pepper in a small bowl. Pat onto the cut sides of the salmon. Let the salmon stand for 5 minutes.

Preheat the grill to High. Place the grill rack 5 inches above the coals and coat the rack with oil.

Grill the salmon, rub side down, for 4 minutes, watching closely to prevent overcooking. Turn the salmon over carefully and cook for 4 to 5 minutes longer or until seared on the outside but a little cool at the center. Serve with grilled vegetables or a salad.

Pan-Seared Salmon with Mushrooms and Spinach

Nonstick cooking spray

4 (6-ounce) 1-inch-thick salmon fillets

½ teaspoon salt, divided

¼ teaspoon black pepper

1 teaspoon olive oil

1 tablespoon thinly sliced shallots

1½ cups presliced mushrooms

2 cups fresh spinach

1 teaspoon grated lemon peel

1 teaspoon fresh lemon juice

Spray a large nonstick skillet with cooking spray and place over medium-high heat. Sprinkle the salmon with ¼ teaspoon of the salt and pepper. Add the salmon to the skillet and cook for 5 minutes per side or until the salmon flakes easily with a fork. Remove the salmon from the pan; keep warm.

Add the olive oil and shallots to the pan and sauté for 1 minute. Add the mushrooms in a single layer and cook for 2 minutes (do not stir). Cook for 2 minutes longer, stirring frequently. Add the spinach and cook for 30 seconds or until the spinach is wilted. Remove from the heat and stir in the remaining salt, lemon peel and lemon juice. Serve over the salmon.

Roasted Salmon

Vicki Gay's great salmon! It is so good!

¼ cup pineapple juice

2 tablespoons fresh lemon juice

4 (6-ounce) 1-inch salmon fillets

    Nonstick cooking spray

2 tablespoons brown sugar

4 teaspoons chili powder

2 teaspoons lemon zest

¾ teaspoon ground cumin

½ teaspoon salt

¼ teaspoon cinnamon

Combine the pineapple juice, lemon juice and salmon in a resealable plastic bag. Marinate in the refrigerator for 1 hour, turning occasionally.

Preheat the oven to 400 degrees. Spray an 11x17-inch baking dish with cooking spray. Remove the salmon from the bag, discarding the marinade. Combine the brown sugar, chili powder, lemon zest, cumin, salt and cinnamon in a bowl and mix well. Rub over the salmon and place in the prepared baking dish. Bake for 15 to 20 minutes or until the salmon flakes easily with a fork. Serve with lemon slices.

Mediterranean-Style Penne

8 slices of bacon, chopped

1 large onion, chopped

1 small eggplant, diced

2 cups chopped tomatoes

4 large garlic cloves, chopped

1 tablespoon red wine vinegar

1 teaspoon dried thyme, finely crumbled

⅓ cup drained capers, rinsed

    Salt and pepper to taste

1 pound penne, cooked

2 tablespoons olive oil

1½ cups (about 7 ounces) crumbled feta cheese

½ cup pitted kalamata olives

    Chopped Italian parsley

Cook the bacon in a large heavy skillet over medium-high heat until crisp. Transfer the bacon to paper towels using a slotted spoon. Add the onion and eggplant. Sauté for 15 minutes or until tender. Add the tomatoes, garlic, vinegar and thyme. Reduce the heat to medium and cook for 5 minutes. Stir in the capers, salt and pepper. Toss the pasta with the olive oil in a large bowl. Stir in the eggplant mixture, cheese, olives and bacon. Sprinkle with parsley.

Kristin's Stuffed Shells

Kristin is Stephanie's daughter-in-law and is a great cook. When the family is together, this is what they request.

SHELLS

1 package jumbo pasta shells

2 eggs

15 ounces ricotta cheese

½ teaspoon chopped parsley

Dash of salt and pepper

1 cup mozzarella cheese, divided

1 (26-ounce) jar marinara sauce (we prefer Rao's Arrabbiata sauce for a little kick)

CHEESY BREAD

1 loaf French bread

3 garlic cloves

4 tablespoons butter, melted

1 cup mascarpone cheese

Chopped fresh parsley

Preheat the oven to 350 degrees.

For the Shells, cook the pasta according to package directions; drain. Rinse the pasta in a colander. Drain well and place in a bowl.

Mix the eggs, ricotta cheese, parsley, salt, pepper and half of the mozzarella cheese in a bowl. Spread a small amount of the marinara sauce over the bottom of a 9x13-inch baking dish. Spoon the cheese mixture into the shells and place the shells in the dish. Pour the remaining marinara sauce over the shells and sprinkle with the remaining mozzarella cheese. Bake, covered with foil, for 30 minutes. Bake, uncovered, for 10 minutes or until the cheese is melted.

Meanwhile, for the Cheesy Bread, cut the bread lengthwise into halves and place on a baking sheet. Press the garlic into the butter using a garlic press and mix well. Spread the garlic butter over the cut sides of the bread. Spread with the cheese. Bake for 15 minutes or until the crust is golden brown and the cheese is bubbly. Sprinkle with the parsley.

Serve the shells with the Cheesy Bread and a salad, and you have a perfect meal the whole family will love.

Pasta with Tomatoes and Mascarpone Cheese

1 (24-ounce) package frozen cheese-filled ravioli

3 pints assorted grape tomatoes

1 large tomato, chopped

2 garlic cloves, chopped

2 tablespoons olive oil

4 tablespoons butter, cubed

1 tablespoon fresh lemon juice

¾ teaspoon kosher salt

¼ teaspoon freshly ground black pepper

½ cup torn assorted fresh herbs such as parsley and basil, divided

8 ounces mascarpone cheese

Cook the ravioli according to package directions; drain. Place in a large serving bowl.

Meanwhile, preheat the broiler with the oven rack 4 to 5 inches from the heat source.

Stir the grape tomatoes, tomato, garlic and olive oil in a medium bowl. Pour into a 10x15-inch jelly roll pan. Broil for 5 to 8 minutes or until the tomatoes are charred, stirring halfway through.

Transfer the tomato mixture to a bowl. Stir in the butter, lemon juice, salt, pepper and ¼ cup of the herbs. Spoon over the hot ravioli and dollop with the cheese. Sprinkle with the remaining fresh herbs and serve immediately.

Garlic Honey Marinade for Chicken

1 small onion, minced

¼ cup fresh lemon juice

¼ cup sesame oil

2 tablespoons light soy sauce

2 garlic cloves, crushed

1 tablespoon grated fresh ginger

2 tablespoons honey

2 teaspoons chopped fresh parsley

Combine the onion, lemon juice, sesame oil, soy sauce, garlic, ginger, honey and parsley in a bowl. Marinate the chicken in the marinade for 8 hours or overnight.

Dumplings with Soy Slaw

2 (9-ounce) packages fresh or frozen dumplings or potstickers

¼ cup rice vinegar

3 teaspoons sugar

2 teaspoons soy sauce

¼ cup water

Hot sauce to taste (optional)

1 (16-ounce) package coleslaw mix

5 scallions, thinly sliced on the diagonal

¼ cup roasted peanuts

Cook the dumplings according to the package directions (pan-frying is preferable to steaming). Meanwhile, combine the vinegar, sugar, soy sauce, water and hot sauce in a large bowl and mix well. Add the coleslaw mix and toss to coat.

Divide the slaw among individual bowls and sprinkle with the scallions and peanuts. Top with the cooked dumplings. Pour any sauce that remains in the bowl over the dumplings. Serve with soy sauce on the side.

Slow Cooker Red Beans and Rice

3 cups water

1 cup dried pinto beans

1 cup chopped onion

1 cup chopped green bell pepper

¾ cup chopped celery

1 teaspoon dried thyme

1 teaspoon paprika

¾ teaspoon ground red pepper

½ teaspoon black pepper

½ (14-ounce) package turkey, pork and beef smoked sausage, thinly sliced (such as Healthy Choice)

1 bay leaf

5 garlic cloves, minced

1 teaspoon salt

3 cups hot cooked long-grain rice

¼ cup chopped green onions for garnish

Combine the water, pinto beans, onion, bell pepper, celery, thyme, paprika, red pepper, black pepper, sausage, bay leaf and garlic in a slow cooker. Cook, covered, on High for 5 hours. Discard the bay leaf and stir in the salt. Serve over the rice and sprinkle with green onions.

NOTE: May replace some of the water with a can of stewed tomatoes.

Best Friends

Ruidoso, New Mexico

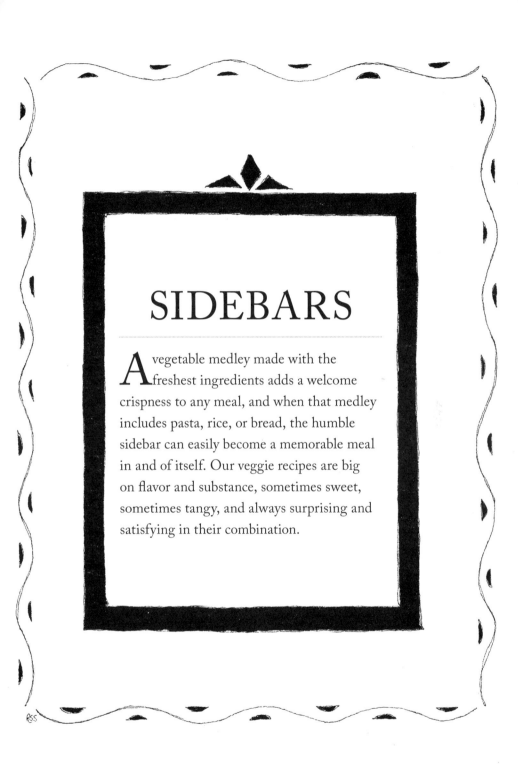

SIDEBARS

A vegetable medley made with the freshest ingredients adds a welcome crispness to any meal, and when that medley includes pasta, rice, or bread, the humble sidebar can easily become a memorable meal in and of itself. Our veggie recipes are big on flavor and substance, sometimes sweet, sometimes tangy, and always surprising and satisfying in their combination.

Asparagus Oriental

1½ pounds fresh asparagus

1 tablespoon vegetable oil

1½ teaspoons reduced-sodium
   soy sauce

1 teaspoon sesame oil

1 teaspoon water

1 garlic clove, pressed

¼ teaspoon ground ginger

1 tablespoon sesame seeds,
   toasted

Steam the asparagus in a steamer for 8 to 10 minutes or until crisp-tender. Remove to a serving dish.

Mix the vegetable oil, soy sauce, sesame oil, water, garlic and ginger in a bowl and pour over the asparagus. Marinate at room temperature or in the refrigerator for 1 hour or longer.

Serve cold or reheat in the microwave. Sprinkle with the sesame seeds just before serving.

Asparagus with Pecans and Bacon

1 tablespoon olive oil

Nonstick cooking spray

1 tablespoon minced fresh garlic

1½ pounds asparagus, cut into 1½-inch pieces

2 tablespoons balsamic vinegar

2 teaspoons sugar

1½ teaspoons minced fresh tarragon

¾ teaspoon salt

⅛ teaspoon freshly ground black pepper

2 tablespoons chopped pecans, toasted

2 slices of bacon, cooked and crumbled

Heat the olive oil in a large nonstick skillet coated with cooking spray over medium-high heat. Add the garlic and sauté for 1 minute. Add the asparagus; sauté for 4 minutes or until tender.

Mix the vinegar and sugar in a small bowl. Drizzle over the asparagus. Stir in the tarragon, salt and pepper. Cook for 2 minutes, stirring frequently. Spoon into a serving dish. Sprinkle with the pecans and bacon.

NOTE: To toast pecans, spread on a baking sheet and bake at 350 degrees for 8 to 10 minutes.

Grilled Asparagus with Gorgonzola Butter

¾ cup crumbled Gorgonzola cheese

6 tablespoons butter, softened

1 teaspoon fresh lemon juice

Salt and pepper to taste

2 tablespoons olive oil

1 tablespoon fresh basil

3 garlic cloves, minced

2 pounds asparagus, trimmed

Combine the cheese, butter and lemon juice in a medium bowl and stir to blend. Season with salt and pepper. Cover and refrigerate the Gorgonzola butter for up to 2 days.

Preheat the grill to High.

Whisk the olive oil, basil and garlic in a small bowl until blended. Arrange the asparagus in a single layer in a baking dish. Pour the olive oil mixture over the asparagus and turn to coat. Sprinkle with salt and pepper. Grill the asparagus for 4 minutes or until charred on all sides, turning occasionally. Transfer to a plate. Top the asparagus with the desired amount of the Gorgonzola butter and serve.

A strong friendship doesn't need daily conversations, doesn't always need togetherness. As long as the relationship lives in the heart, true friends will never part.

UNKNOWN

Madelyn's Favorite Broccoli Pasta

Madelyn is Stephanie's granddaughter, and she requests that her mom make this dish very often!

16 ounces penne pasta

3 garlic cloves, minced

2 broccoli crowns, chopped

⅓ cup olive oil

½ cup chicken broth

⅓ cup freshly grated Romano cheese

Cook the pasta according to the package directions. Sauté the garlic and broccoli in the olive oil in a skillet until tender. Add the pasta, broth and cheese; stir to mix well. Serve with additional cheese.

Serve with fresh fruit and your kids' favorite chicken, and you'll have a great meal they will love.

NOTE: You may substitute mozzarella cheese for the Romano cheese.

Mustard-Glazed Baby Carrots

3 (16-ounce) packages peeled baby carrots

1 cup water

2 tablespoons butter

⅓ cup country mustard

¼ cup packed brown sugar

⅓ cup chopped walnuts, toasted

½ cup loosely packed fresh parsley leaves, chopped

Bring the carrots and water to a boil in a large saucepan over medium-high heat. Reduce the heat to low. Cover and simmer for 15 minutes or until the carrots are crisp-tender; drain.

Return the carrots to the saucepan. Add the butter, mustard and brown sugar. Cook over medium heat for 10 minutes or until the carrots are tender and well coated, stirring occasionally.

Spoon the carrots into a serving dish and sprinkle with the walnuts and parsley leaves.

Roasted Broccoli with Chipotle Honey Butter

This will make your Sunday barbecues a hit! And your kids will eat their veggies with the honey butter!

- 2 pounds broccoli
- 4 tablespoons unsalted butter, melted
- 3 garlic cloves, minced
- 2 chipotle peppers in adobo sauce (use less if you don't want the dish spicy)
- 1 tablespoon honey
- 1 teaspoon salt
- 2 teaspoons fresh lime juice (about 2 limes)

Preheat the oven to 450 degrees. Line a baking sheet with aluminum foil to make cleaning easier.

Cut the broccoli into 2-inch florets, leaving one to two inches of stems attached. Combine the butter, garlic, chipotle peppers, honey and salt in a large bowl; mix well. Add the broccoli and toss to coat evenly.

Transfer the broccoli mixture to the prepared baking sheet. Roast for 12 minutes or until the broccoli is crisp-tender and lightly browned in spots, turning occasionally. Sprinkle the lime juice over the top. Transfer the broccoli mixture to a serving dish, scraping up any bits of garlic and chipotle peppers using a rubber spatula. Toss to mix.

Corn and Okra Medley

4 ears of fresh corn

8 ounces fresh okra

4 slices of bacon, chopped

1 small onion, chopped

½ cup water

1 to 1½ teaspoons chili powder

1 teaspoon beef bouillon granules

4 medium tomatoes, peeled and chopped

Cut the corn from the cobs and slice the okra. Set aside.

Cook the bacon in a large skillet over medium heat until crisp; remove the bacon using a slotted spoon, reserving the drippings in the skillet. Add the corn, okra, onion, water, chili powder and bouillon to the drippings. Bring to a boil; cover. Reduce the heat and cook for 10 minutes, stirring occasionally.

Stir in the tomatoes; cover and cook for 5 minutes. Stir in the bacon.

Green Bean and Corn Casserole

1 can French-style green beans, drained

1 can white whole kernel corn, drained

1 can cream of celery soup

½ cup sour cream

⅓ cup chopped onion

½ to 1 cup shredded Cheddar cheese

1 sleeve Ritz crackers, crushed

½ cup butter, melted

Preheat the oven to 350 degrees. Grease a casserole dish.

Layer the green beans and corn in the prepared casserole dish. Combine the soup, sour cream, onion and cheese in a bowl and mix well. Pour over the layers. Top with the crackers and drizzle with the butter. Bake for 45 minutes.

Green Beans with Caramelized Red Onions

6 tablespoons olive oil, divided

1½ pounds red onions, thinly sliced

Salt and pepper

1 pound slender green beans, trimmed

1½ tablespoons balsamic vinegar

¾ teaspoon dried tarragon

Heat 3 tablespoons of the olive oil in a large heavy skillet over medium-high heat. Add the onions and sauté for 35 minutes or until dark brown. Season with salt and pepper. Cook the green beans in a medium saucepan of boiling salted water for 4 minutes or just until crisp-tender; drain. Rinse with cold water until cool; pat dry.

Whisk the remaining olive oil, vinegar and tarragon in a large bowl to blend. Add the green beans and onions and toss to coat. Season with salt and pepper. Serve warm or at room temperature.

Green Beans with Honey Cashew Sauce

½ cup coarsely chopped salted cashews

3 tablespoons unsalted butter

2 tablespoons honey

1 pound fresh green beans

Sauté the cashews in the butter in a skillet over low heat for 5 minutes. Add the honey and cook for 1 minute, stirring constantly.

Blanch the green beans to al dente and drain. Pour the sauce over the green beans in a bowl and toss to coat.

Mediterranean Green Beans

1 pound fresh French-style green beans, trimmed

8 ounces fresh mushrooms, sliced

2 tablespoons olive oil

2 tablespoons balsamic vinegar

Salt and fresh ground black pepper to taste

2 tablespoons fresh finely grated Parmesan cheese

Preheat the oven to 375 degrees. Combine the green beans and mushrooms in a plastic bowl or 1-gallon resealable plastic bag. Whisk together the olive oil and vinegar in a small bowl and pour over the green beans and mushrooms. Stir until the green beans and mushrooms are lightly coated. Spread in a single layer on a large baking sheet; do not overcrowd. Roast for 20 to 30 minutes or until the green beans are crisp-tender. Season with salt and pepper and sprinkle with the cheese. Serve hot.

NOTE: Fresh French-style green beans may be found in a plastic bag in the fresh produce section of the grocery store.

Eating is a necessity, but cooking is an art.
UNKNOWN

Andouille and White Cheddar–Stuffed Potatoes

Can be a meal by itself!

8 large baking potatoes	½ cup butter
Olive oil to taste	1½ cups crème fraîche
Salt and freshly ground black pepper to taste	8 ounces white Cheddar cheese, grated, divided
3 tablespoons olive oil, divided	¼ cup chopped chives
2 cups thinly sliced onions	¼ cup chopped parsley
8 ounces andouille sausage links, finely chopped	

Preheat the oven to 400 degrees. Season the potatoes with olive oil, salt and pepper to taste. Place on a baking sheet and bake for 1 hour or until tender. Remove from the oven and cool.

Heat 2 tablespoons of the olive oil in a sauté pan over medium heat. Add the onions. Season with salt and pepper. Cook for 8 minutes or until caramelized, stirring frequently. Remove from the heat and cool.

Meanwhile, heat the remaining olive oil in a sauté pan over medium heat. Add the sausage and cook until brown, stirring frequently. Remove the sausage using a slotted spoon; drain on paper towels. Set aside.

Cut off and discard the top fourth of each potato. Remove the pulp from each potato using a slotted spoon, leaving ¼-inch-thick shells. Combine the potato pulp, butter and crème fraîche in a bowl. Season with salt and pepper. Mash until smooth. Add half the cheese, the sausage, chives and parsley and mix well.

Fill each potato shell with potato mixture. Top with the remaining cheese. Place on a baking sheet and bake until the potatoes are warm and the cheese is melted. Remove from the oven and serve hot.

Grilled Potatoes

3 tablespoons Dijon mustard

3 tablespoons olive oil

⅛ teaspoon garlic powder

¼ teaspoon salt

¾ teaspoon Italian seasoning

4 medium peeled or unpeeled potatoes, cut into chunks

Combine the mustard, olive oil, garlic, salt and Italian seasoning in a small bowl and mix well. Pour over the potatoes in a large bowl and toss to coat.

Preheat the grill to Medium-High. Place the potatoes on a vegetable grilling rack. Grill for 20 to 30 minutes, turning once halfway through.

Loaded Potato Casserole

6 unpeeled russet potatoes, cut into ¼-inch slices

Salt and pepper to taste

1 cup shredded Cheddar cheese

1 cup shredded Monterey Jack cheese

8 slices of bacon, cooked and crumbled

2 cups milk

2 large eggs

Fresh or dried parsley for garnish

Preheat the oven to 375 degrees. Butter a 9x13-inch casserole dish.

Layer half of the potato slices in the dish, overlapping slightly. Season with salt and pepper. Sprinkle the Cheddar cheese, Monterey Jack cheese and bacon over the potatoes. Layer with the remaining potato slices.

Mix the milk and eggs in a small bowl. Pour over the potatoes. Garnish with the parsley. Cover with foil and bake for 90 minutes or until the custard is cooked and set. Let stand, uncovered, for 15 to 20 minutes before serving.

Twice-Baked Potato Casserole

This will be the best potato casserole you have ever eaten, or maybe the Loaded Potato Casserole will be!

5 pounds new potatoes

1 pound bacon, diced

12 ounces cream cheese

4 ounces chives, cut into ¼-inch pieces

1 tablespoon salt

1½ teaspoons ground black pepper

½ cup butter, melted

1 cup half-and-half

12 ounces sour cream

Whole milk (optional)

2 cups shredded Cheddar Jack cheese blend

Wash the potatoes and cut into halves. Place in a saucepan and cover with water. Bring to a boil over medium-high heat. Boil until the potatoes are tender. Drain immediately to prevent overcooking and water absorption.

Meanwhile, cook the bacon in a saucepan until medium-well; drain.

Combine the cream cheese, chives, salt, pepper, butter, half-and-half and sour cream in a bowl and mix well.

Preheat the oven to 350 degrees. Grease an 11x13-inch baking dish.

Combine the potatoes, cream cheese mixture and bacon in a bowl and mix well, adding whole milk if the mixture is too thick. Spoon into the prepared baking dish; sprinkle with the cheese. Bake for 45 minutes.

The best things in life are the people we love, the places we've been, and the memories we've made along the way.

UNKNOWN

Rosemary Roasted Potatoes with Goat Cheese

10 cups cubed potatoes (about 4 pounds)

2 tablespoons chopped fresh rosemary, or 2 teaspoons dried rosemary

3 tablespoons balsamic vinegar

1 tablespoon olive oil

½ teaspoon salt

¼ teaspoon pepper

6 garlic cloves, chopped

Nonstick cooking spray

¾ cup crumbled goat cheese (about 3 ounces)

Preheat the oven to 400 degrees. Combine the potatoes, rosemary, vinegar, olive oil, salt, pepper and garlic in a large resealable plastic bag, turning to coat well.

Arrange the potatoes on a large baking pan coated with cooking spray. Bake for 45 minutes or until brown. Place in a large bowl; sprinkle with the cheese and toss to mix well.

Smashed Potatoes

These potatoes have a great crunch as well as a soft center. Really good!

12 new red potatoes

Olive oil

Salt and pepper to taste

2 to 3 garlic cloves, minced

Fresh herbs to taste

½ cup Parmesan cheese, grated

Combine the potatoes with enough water to cover in a saucepan. Bring to a boil and cook until tender.

Preheat the oven to 450 degrees. Drizzle olive oil on a large baking pan. Arrange the potatoes on the pan and smash with a potato masher, rotating the masher back and forth. Drizzle with olive oil. Sprinkle with salt, pepper, garlic and herbs if desired. Top with the Parmesan cheese. Bake for 20 minutes.

Acorn Squash with Cranberry and Mushroom Stuffing

2 small acorn squash, cut lengthwise into halves and seeded

Olive oil

1 cup dried cranberries

4 tablespoons unsalted butter, divided

¼ cup minced shallots

1 teaspoon minced garlic

¼ cup chopped shiitake mushroom caps

¾ cup chopped button or cremini mushrooms

1 tablespoon grated lemon zest

½ teaspoon dried Mexican oregano

2 cups fresh breadcrumbs

Vegetable stock

½ teaspoon salt

¼ teaspoon pepper

Preheat the oven to 425 degrees. Brush the cut sides of the squash lightly with olive oil. Arrange cut side down on a baking sheet. Bake for 20 minutes or just until tender.

Place the cranberries in a microwave-safe bowl and add enough water to cover. Microwave on High for 4 minutes. Let stand until cool; drain.

Melt 2 tablespoons of the butter in a heavy skillet over medium heat. Add the shallots and garlic and sauté for 3 to 4 minutes or until tender. Add the shiitake and button mushrooms, lemon zest and oregano. Sauté for 3 to 4 minutes or until the mushrooms are tender. Add the breadcrumbs and cook until light brown, stirring constantly. Stir in the cranberries. Stir in enough stock to moisten. Stir in the salt and pepper.

Spoon into the squash and place squash upright on the baking sheet. Dot with the remaining butter. Bake for 10 to 15 minutes or until heated through and brown.

Butternut Squash and Rice Pilaf

1 teaspoon olive oil

1 cup chopped onion

3 garlic cloves, minced

3 cups peeled and cubed
(½ inch) butternut squash
or other winter squash
(about 1 pound)

2 cups water

1 cup uncooked long-grain rice

½ cup chopped bottled roasted
red peppers

1 teaspoon dried rubbed sage

1 teaspoon lemon juice

½ teaspoon salt

½ teaspoon ground cumin

¼ teaspoon black pepper

Heat the olive oil in a large saucepan over medium heat. Add the onion and garlic and sauté for 3 minutes. Add the squash, water and rice and mix well. Bring to a boil. Cover and reduce the heat. Simmer for 20 minutes or until the liquid is absorbed, stirring occasionally. Stir in the roasted red peppers, sage, lemon juice, salt, cumin and pepper.

Squash and Rice Casserole

8 cups sliced zucchini (about
2½ pounds)

1 cup chopped onion

½ cup fat-free, reduced-sodium
chicken broth

2 cups cooked rice

1 cup fat-free sour cream

1 cup shredded reduced-fat
sharp Cheddar cheese

4 tablespoons grated fresh
Parmesan cheese, divided

¼ cup Italian-style breadcrumbs

1 teaspoon salt

¼ teaspoon black pepper

2 large eggs, lightly beaten

Nonstick cooking spray

Combine the zucchini, onion and broth in a Dutch oven; bring to a boil. Cover and reduce the heat. Simmer for 20 minutes or until tender, stirring frequently; drain. Mash the mixture coarsely using a potato masher.

Preheat the oven to 350 degrees. Combine the zucchini mixture, rice, sour cream, Cheddar cheese, 2 tablespoons Parmesan cheese, breadcrumbs, salt, pepper and eggs in a bowl; stir gently. Spoon into a 9x13-inch baking dish coated with cooking spray; sprinkle with the remaining Parmesan cheese. Bake for 30 minutes or until bubbly.

Squash Strudel

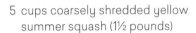

5 cups coarsely shredded yellow summer squash (1½ pounds)

5 cups coarsely shredded zucchini (1½ pounds)

½ teaspoon salt

8 eggs, beaten

2 tablespoons snipped fresh parsley, or 2 teaspoons dried parsley flakes

2 garlic cloves, minced

1 tablespoon finely chopped onion, or ½ teaspoon minced dried onion

1 tablespoon snipped fresh dill, or ½ teaspoon dried dill weed

¼ teaspoon pepper

8 ounces crumbled feta cheese

5 sheets frozen phyllo dough, thawed

4 tablespoons butter, melted

Combine the yellow squash, zucchini and salt in a large bowl. Let stand for 15 minutes. Place in a colander and press to drain.

Preheat the oven to 350 degrees. Combine the eggs, parsley, garlic, onion, dill and pepper in a large bowl. Stir in the squash mixture and cheese. Spoon evenly into a 9x13-inch baking pan.

Cut the phyllo sheets crosswise into halves. Brush a sheet of phyllo lightly with butter and place over the squash mixture. Top with another sheet of phyllo. Brush with more butter. Add the remaining phyllo sheets, brushing each sheet with butter. Score through the phyllo layers using a sharp knife, making 16 squares.

Bake for 50 to 55 minutes or until a knife inserted near the center comes out clean, covering with foil for the last 10 minutes of baking to prevent overbrowning. Let stand for 10 minutes before serving.

Squash Sauté

1 tablespoon vegetable oil

¾ cup red bell pepper strips

½ cup sliced onion, separated
into rings

2 garlic cloves, crushed

1¾ cups sliced zucchini

1½ cups sliced yellow squash

1¾ cups plum tomatoes

¼ cup thinly sliced fresh basil

1 teaspoon lemon pepper

¼ teaspoon salt

¾ cup grated Parmesan cheese

Heat the vegetable oil in a large nonstick skillet over high heat for 2 minutes.
Add the bell pepper, onion, garlic, zucchini and yellow squash and sauté for
5 minutes or until the vegetables are crisp-tender. Add the tomatoes, basil,
lemon pepper and salt. Remove from the heat. Sprinkle with the cheese and
serve immediately.

Bourbon Sweet Potatoes

6 medium sweet potatoes

½ cup chopped pecans

6 tablespoons butter, melted

½ cup firmly packed brown sugar

½ cup orange juice

½ cup bourbon

½ teaspoon ground cinnamon

¼ teaspoon ground cloves

¼ teaspoon ground nutmeg

Chopped pecans for garnish

Bring the sweet potatoes and enough water to cover to a boil in a large Dutch
oven over high heat. Reduce the heat; cook for 30 to 45 minutes or just until
the sweet potatoes are tender. Drain and let stand to cool.

Preheat the oven to 350 degrees. Grease a 9x13-inch baking dish lightly.

Peel the sweet potatoes. Cut off and discard the ends. Cut the sweet
potatoes into 1-inch-thick rounds. Arrange evenly in the prepared baking dish.
Sprinkle evenly with the pecans.

Combine the butter, brown sugar, orange juice, bourbon, cinnamon, cloves
and nutmeg in a bowl and mix well. Pour evenly over the sweet potatoes.

Bake for 25 minutes or until heated through. Garnish with pecans.

Cranberry Orange Chutney

Great holiday side dish or as a relish on turkey sandwiches.

4 cups fresh cranberries	1¾ to 2 cups sugar
1 orange, peeled and chopped	½ cup orange juice
1 unpeeled apple, chopped	½ teaspoon ground ginger
½ cup raisins	½ teaspoon ground cinnamon
⅓ cup chopped pecans	1 tablespoon vinegar

Combine the cranberries, orange, apple, raisins, pecans, sugar, orange juice, ginger, cinnamon and vinegar in a saucepan. Bring to a boil. Simmer for 5 to 8 minutes or until the cranberries begin to pop, stirring occasionally.

Mixed Vegetable Pasta

6 ounces spaghetti	1 cup sliced fresh mushrooms
1 tablespoon olive oil	1 small tomato, chopped
2 tablespoons chicken or vegetable broth	2 tablespoons white wine
1 cup broccoli florets	2 tablespoons grated Parmesan cheese
1 cup thinly sliced carrots	1 tablespoon minced fresh parsley
1 cup sliced zucchini	1 teaspoon red pepper flakes
1 cup sliced onion	
1 small yellow bell pepper, cut into strips	

Cook the pasta according to the package directions; drain. Set aside.

Coat a large nonstick skillet with olive oil. Place over medium heat until hot. Add the broth, broccoli, carrots, zucchini and onion and sauté for 4 minutes. Add the bell pepper and mushrooms and sauté for 4 minutes. Add the pasta, tomato and wine and toss gently. Cook until thoroughly heated, stirring occasionally. Spoon into a serving bowl. Sprinkle immediately with the cheese, parsley and pepper flakes and toss gently to mix. Serve immediately.

NOTE: May use whole wheat spaghetti.

Garlic Cheese Grits

2 cups water
2 cups heavy cream
1 cup yellow grits
¾ teaspoon salt

½ tablespoon chopped garlic
½ cup unsalted butter
½ cup grated Parmesan cheese

Combine the water, cream, grits, salt and garlic in a medium saucepan. Cook, uncovered, until thick and creamy, stirring occasionally. Stir in the butter and cheese just before serving. Serve hot.

Mushroom Wild Rice

4 cups water
1 cup wild rice
1 teaspoon butter
1 teaspoon salt
½ cup brown rice
8 slices of bacon, chopped
2 cups sliced fresh mushrooms

1 onion, chopped
1 green bell pepper, chopped
1 red bell pepper, chopped
1 rib of celery, chopped
1 can beef broth
2 tablespoons cornstarch
¼ cup cold water

Bring the water, wild rice, butter and salt to a boil in a large saucepan. Reduce the heat. Cover and simmer for 40 minutes. Stir in the brown rice. Cover and simmer for 25 to 30 minutes or until the rice is tender.

Meanwhile, cook the bacon in a large skillet until crisp. Remove the bacon to paper towels to drain, reserving 2 tablespoons drippings in the skillet.

Preheat the oven to 350 degrees. Grease a 9x13-inch baking dish.

Sauté the mushrooms, onion, green pepper, red pepper and celery in the reserved drippings until tender. Stir in the broth. Bring to a boil. Combine the cornstarch and water in a small bowl and stir until smooth. Stir into the mushroom mixture. Cook for 2 minutes or until thickened and bubbly, stirring constantly; stir in bacon.

Drain the rice; add the mushroom mixture and mix well. Spoon into the prepared baking dish. Cover and bake for 25 minutes. Uncover and bake for 5 to 10 minutes longer or until heated through.

Risotto with Vegetables

1 medium-size purple onion	16 ounces arborio rice
1 medium-size yellow squash	4 (14-ounce) cans reduced-
3 medium-size yellow, red or green bell peppers	sodium fat-free chicken broth
2 medium carrots	½ teaspoon salt
2 garlic cloves, minced	½ teaspoon ground black pepper
1 tablespoon olive oil	¾ teaspoon ground white pepper
1 tablespoon chopped fresh rosemary	

Cut the onion, squash, bell peppers and carrots into thin strips.

Sauté the vegetables and garlic in the hot olive oil in a Dutch oven over medium-high heat until tender; stir in the rosemary. Remove to a plate using a slotted spoon. Set aside.

Add the rice to the Dutch oven and sauté for 5 minutes. Reduce the heat to medium. Add 1 cup of the chicken broth and cook until the liquid is absorbed, stirring constantly. Repeat the procedure with the remaining broth, using 1 cup at a time. (Total cooking time should be about 30 minutes.) Stir in the salt, black pepper and white pepper. Spoon into a serving dish; top with the vegetables.

Spinach and Mushroom Risotto

½ (10-ounce) package frozen spinach

4 cups reduced-sodium fat-free chicken broth

1½ teaspoons olive oil

1 tablespoon unsalted butter

1 cup chopped onion

1 cup sliced fresh mushrooms

1 garlic clove, minced

1 cup arborio or other short-grain rice

3 tablespoons white wine

¼ cup grated Parmesan cheese

½ teaspoon kosher salt

¼ teaspoon freshly ground pepper

Cook the spinach according to the package directions. Drain, squeezing out as much water as possible. Chop the spinach. Heat the broth in a saucepan.

Heat the olive oil and butter in a 2- or 3-quart heavy pot until the butter is melted. Add the onion, mushrooms and garlic. Cook for 3 minutes or until the vegetables are golden brown. Add the rice and cook until the rice is shiny, stirring constantly. Stir in the wine.

Add 1 cup of the broth and bring to a boil. Reduce the heat and simmer until almost all of the broth is absorbed, stirring constantly. Add ½ cup broth and cook until the broth is absorbed, stirring constantly. Repeat the procedure for 20 to 25 minutes or until all the broth is used and the rice is creamy on the outside but still a bit firm to the bite. Stir in the cheese, salt, pepper and spinach.

Rice and Green Chile Casserole

1 cup rice

3 tablespoons butter, divided

2 cups sour cream

1 (4-ounce) can chopped green chilies

8 ounces Monterey Jack cheese, cut into strips

Salt and pepper to taste

½ cup shredded sharp Cheddar cheese (optional)

Cook the rice according to the package directions just until tender. Stir in 1 tablespoon of the butter.

Preheat the oven to 350 degrees. Butter a casserole dish.

Layer half the rice, ⅓ of the sour cream, half the chilies and half the Monterey Jack cheese in the prepared casserole dish. Season with salt and pepper. Repeat the layers of rice, sour cream, chilies and Monterey Jack cheese. Spread with the remaining sour cream. Dot with the remaining butter and sprinkle with the Cheddar cheese. Bake for 30 minutes or until browned.

Broccoli Cornbread

This bread is so moist; it reheats well. So you can make it a day in advance, store it in the refrigerator and then either warm it in the oven or just bring it to room temperature. Great paired with soup!

2 (8-ounce) boxes corn muffin mix

1 cup butter, melted

4 eggs, beaten

1 cup cottage cheese

1 cup finely chopped onion (1 medium)

1 (10-ounce) package frozen chopped broccoli, thawed and excess water squeezed out

Preheat the oven to 350 degrees. Grease a 9x13-inch baking pan.

Combine the corn muffin mix, butter, eggs, cottage cheese, onion and broccoli in a bowl and mix well. Spoon into the prepared baking pan. Bake for 35 to 40 minutes or until the edges are lightly browned and a wooden pick inserted near the center comes out clean. Cut into squares to serve.

Cornbread Vegetable Bake

1½ cups fine-ground white cornmeal

1½ teaspoons salt, divided

1 teaspoon baking powder

2 eggs

1¾ cups buttermilk or soured milk

1 cup fresh corn kernels

1 cup (about 4 ounces) thinly sliced okra

1 medium onion, finely chopped (about 1 cup)

½ teaspoon freshly ground black pepper

2 tablespoons unsalted butter

Preheat the oven to 450 degrees. Mix the cornmeal, 1 teaspoon of the salt and baking powder in a bowl. Beat the eggs lightly in a small bowl. Stir in the buttermilk. Pour over the cornmeal mixture, stirring to make a smooth, glossy batter. Combine the corn, okra, onion, pepper and the remaining salt in a bowl and mix well. Stir into the batter.

Cut the butter into pieces and put the pieces in a 10-inch cast-iron skillet or baking pan. Heat the skillet in the oven until the butter is melted and foaming. Remove from the oven and swirl the butter to coat the bottom and sides of the pan. Add the butter to the batter and stir to mix. Pour the batter into the hot skillet. Bake for 40 to 50 minutes or until golden brown. Invert the cornbread onto a serving plate. Let stand to cool for 5 minutes. Cut into wedges and serve hot.

NOTES: You may substitute yellow cornmeal, but white cornmeal is more traditionally Southern. Frozen corn kernels, thawed and drained, may be used. No buttermilk? To sour milk, stir together 1¾ cups sweet milk, 2 teaspoons lemon juice and 2 teaspoons cider vinegar. Let stand until curdled.

Creamed Corn Biscuits

4 tablespoons butter

1½ cups Bisquick baking mix

1 (8-ounce) can cream-style corn

Dash of cayenne pepper (optional)

Preheat the oven to 375 degrees.

Melt the butter in a jelly roll pan. Combine the Bisquick and corn in a bowl and mix well; the mixture will be thick and sticky. Drop by heaping teaspoonfuls onto the prepared pan. Sprinkle with the cayenne pepper for a little heat. Bake for 15 to 20 minutes or until golden brown.

Diane's Home, Lubbock, Texas

SAVE THE BEST FOR LAST

G ive us more sweets! We always manage to save room for dessert and treasure the discovery of a rich and gooey confection to savor at the end of a gratifying meal. We also love to sneak sweets throughout the day and have included several cookie recipes for snacks or teatime. From deep, dark fudgy cakes to spritely fruit concoctions, we are pleased to share a selection of dessert recipes that will sweeten your friendships and your memories for more good times to come.

Any Day Cake

CAKE

1 egg
½ cup butter, partially melted

1 package cake mix (any flavor; spice cake at Christmas, carrot cake at Easter, etc.)

FILLING

1 (8-ounce) package cream cheese

2 eggs
16 ounces powdered sugar

Preheat the oven to 300 degrees.

For the Cake, beat the egg in a large mixing bowl until creamy. Add the butter and mix well. Add the cake mix and mix thoroughly. Pour into an ungreased 9x13-inch cake pan. Press the mixture over the bottom and 1 inch up the sides of the pan using buttered fingers.

For the Filling, cream the cream cheese, eggs and powdered sugar in a mixing bowl until the mixture looks gooey. Pour over the cake and bake for 45 minutes.

Applesauce Cake

CAKE

3 cups all-purpose flour

1 tablespoon ground cinnamon

1 teaspoon baking soda

2 eggs

1½ cups vegetable oil

2 cups sugar

½ teaspoon salt

16 ounces applesauce

1 teaspoon vanilla extract

1 cup chopped pecans

QUICK CARAMEL ICING

½ cup butter

1 cup brown sugar

¼ cup milk

2 cups powdered sugar, sifted

For the Cake, preheat the oven to 350 degrees. Grease a tube pan or 2 loaf pans.

Combine the flour, cinnamon, baking soda, eggs, vegetable oil, sugar, salt, applesauce and vanilla in a mixing bowl and beat for 3 minutes. Stir in the pecans. Pour into the prepared tube pan or 2 loaf pans and bake for 50 to 60 minutes until a wooden pick inserted in the center comes out clean. Transfer the cake to a wire rack. Let stand to cool.

For the Quick Caramel Icing, melt the butter in a skillet. Add the brown sugar and cook over low heat for 2 minutes, stirring constantly. Stir in the milk. Add the powdered sugar in 3 or 4 portions, stirring constantly. Cook until the icing is the desired consistency, stirring constantly.

Place the cake on a cake plate. Spread the Quick Caramel Icing over the cake.

Chocolate and Peanut Butter Streusel Cake

2¼ cups all-purpose flour

2 cups packed light brown sugar

1 cup creamy peanut butter

½ cup unsalted butter, at room temperature

3 large eggs

1 cup whole milk

1 teaspoon vanilla extract

1 teaspoon baking powder

½ teaspoon baking soda

1 (12-ounce) package semisweet chocolate chips (2 cups), divided

Preheat the oven to 350 degrees. Butter a 9x13-inch cake pan.

Combine the flour, brown sugar, peanut butter and butter in a large bowl. Beat at low speed until the streusel is blended and crumbly. Transfer 1 cup of lightly packed streusel to a small bowl and reserve. Add the eggs, milk, vanilla, baking powder and baking soda to the remaining streusel in the large bowl. Beat at low speed until evenly moist. Increase the speed to medium and beat for 3 minutes or until well blended, scraping the bowl occasionally. Stir in 1 cup of the chocolate chips. Pour the batter into the prepared cake pan. Sprinkle with the reserved streusel and remaining chocolate chips.

Bake the cake for 35 minutes or until a tester inserted into the center comes out clean. Cool the cake in the pan on a wire rack.

 You can't buy happiness but you can buy cake—and that is kind of the same thing.
UNKNOWN

Chocolate Sheath Cake

Most everyone has fond memories of their mother's chocolate cake. Mine would always have it warm when we came home from school. Life doesn't get any better than warm chocolate cake and a glass of milk when you are a kid (or not a kid anymore)!

CAKE

2 cups all-purpose flour

2 cups sugar

1 cup margarine

¼ cup baking cocoa

1 cup water

2 eggs

2 teaspoons vanilla extract

½ cup buttermilk

1 teaspoon baking soda

CHOCOLATE ICING

½ cup butter

¼ cup baking cocoa

¼ cup whole milk

16 ounces powdered sugar

2 teaspoons vanilla extract

For the Cake, preheat the oven to 350 degrees. Grease and flour a large baking dish.

Mix the flour and sugar in a bowl. Melt the margarine in a saucepan. Add the cocoa and water. Bring to a boil, stirring frequently. Add to the flour mixture. Add the eggs, vanilla, buttermilk and baking soda and mix thoroughly. Pour into the prepared baking dish. Bake for 30 minutes.

For the Chocolate Icing, melt the butter in a saucepan. Add the cocoa and milk. Bring to a boil, stirring frequently. Remove from the heat. Add the powdered sugar and vanilla and mix thoroughly.

Spread the Chocolate Icing over the cake.

Cinnamon Roll Cake

CAKE

3 cups all-purpose flour

¼ teaspoon salt

1 cup sugar

4 teaspoons baking powder

1½ cups milk

2 eggs

2 teaspoons vanilla extract

½ cup butter, melted

TOPPING

1 cup butter, softened

1 cup brown sugar

2 tablespoons flour

1 tablespoon ground cinnamon

GLAZE

2 cups powdered sugar

5 tablespoons milk

1 teaspoon vanilla extract

½ cup chopped pecans (optional)

For the Cake, preheat the oven to 350 degrees. Butter a 9x13-inch cake pan.

Combine the flour, salt, sugar, baking powder, milk, eggs, vanilla and butter in a bowl and mix well. Drop by teaspoonfuls as evenly as you can over the entire base of the prepared cake pan.

For the Topping, mix the butter, brown sugar, flour and cinnamon in a bowl. Swirl the topping into the base using a butter knife. Bake for 28 to 30 minutes.

For the Glaze, combine the powdered sugar, milk, vanilla and pecans in a bowl and set aside.

Remove the cake from the oven and pour the glaze over the cake while still warm.

Coconut Cream Cake by Susan Short

1 package white cake mix

1 (8-ounce) can cream of coconut

1 (14-ounce) can of sweetened condensed milk

7 ounces flaked coconut

8 ounces whipping cream

2 to 3 tablespoons sugar

2 ounces toasted flaked coconut for garnish

Bake the cake in a 9x13-inch cake pan according to the package directions. Mix the cream of coconut with the sweetened condensed milk in a bowl. Stir in the coconut.

"Poke a million holes in the cake" using the end of a wooden spoon. Pour the coconut mixture over the cake and refrigerate for several hours or overnight.

Beat the whipping cream at high speed in a mixing bowl until soft peaks form. Add the sugar gradually, beating constantly. Beat until stiff peaks form. Spread over the chilled cake. Garnish with the toasted coconut.

You only live once; lick the bowl.
UNKNOWN

Faye's Carrot Cake

Everyone's got a carrot cake recipe, but this one is special from a special person, Diane's mother-in-law. Diane says, "Best I've ever had." We agree!

CAKE

2 cups sugar

1½ cups vegetable oil

4 eggs

3 cups all-purpose flour

2 teaspoons baking soda

2 teaspoons ground cinnamon

¼ cup buttermilk

½ teaspoon vanilla extract

3 cups grated carrots

CREAM CHEESE FROSTING

½ cup butter, at room
temperature

1 (8-ounce) package cream
cheese, softened

5 cups powdered sugar

1 tablespoon vanilla extract

1 cup chopped pecans

For the Cake, preheat the oven to 325 degrees.

Cream the sugar and vegetable oil in a mixing bowl; beat in the eggs one at a time. Sift the flour, baking soda and cinnamon into a bowl. Add to the egg mixture alternately with the buttermilk and vanilla. Fold in the carrots. Pour into 2 loaf pans and bake for 1 hour. Cool in the pans for 10 minutes. Remove to a wire rack to cool completely.

For the Cream Cheese Frosting, cream the butter and cream cheese in a mixing bowl. Add the powdered sugar and vanilla and mix until smooth. Stir in the pecans.

Spread the Cream Cheese Frosting over the cakes.

Gan-Gan's 7UP Cake

This is Stephanie's mother-in-law's recipe, which her grandchildren requested the most.

3 cups sugar

1 cup butter

½ cup vegetable shortening

5 eggs

3½ cups all-purpose flour

1 cup 7UP

3 teaspoons almond extract

3 teaspoons lemon extract

3 teaspoons vanilla extract

Preheat the oven to 325 degrees. Grease and flour a Bundt pan or angel food cake pan

Cream the sugar, butter and shortening in a mixing bowl. Add the eggs one at a time until thoroughly mixed. Add the flour alternately with the 7UP, mixing thoroughly after each addition. Add the almond extract, lemon extract and vanilla extract and mix well. Pour into the prepared pan and bake for 1 to 1½ hours, checking frequently for doneness using a wooden pick. Let stand to cool completely before removing from the pan.

Lemon Pound Cake with Mint Berries and Lemon Cream

¼ cup sugar

¼ cup loosely packed mint leaves

¾ cup butter, at room temperature

3 cups powdered sugar, divided

3 large eggs

1½ cups all-purpose flour

2½ cups whipping cream, divided

2 teaspoons grated lemon rind

2 tablespoons fresh lemon juice

1 (12-ounce) jar lemon curd

1 quart fresh strawberries, sliced

Fresh mint sprigs for garnish

Preheat the oven to 350 degrees. Grease and flour a 4x8-inch loaf pan.

Process the sugar and mint leaves in a food processor until blended.

Beat the butter at medium speed in a mixing bowl for 2 minutes or until creamy. Add 1½ tablespoons of the mint mixture and 2½ cups of the powdered sugar gradually, beating constantly. Beat for 5 to 7 minutes. Add the eggs one at a time, beating just until the yellow disappears. Add flour alternately with ½ cup of the whipping cream, beginning and ending with flour. Beat at low speed just until blended after each addition. Stir in the lemon rind and lemon juice. Pour the batter into the prepared loaf pan.

Bake at 350 degrees for 1 hour or until a wooden pick inserted in the center comes out clean. Cool in the pan on a wire rack for 10 minutes. Remove the cake from the pan and cool on the wire rack.

For the Lemon Cream, beat the remaining whipping cream, ¼ cup powdered sugar and 1 tablespoon of the mint mixture at medium speed in a mixing bowl until stiff peaks form. Fold in the lemon curd.

For the Mint Berries, stir together the remaining mint mixture, the remaining powdered sugar and the strawberries.

Serve the pound cake with lemon cream and mint strawberries. Garnish with mint sprigs.

Mexican Chocolate Pudding Cake

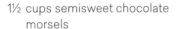

1½ cups semisweet chocolate morsels

½ cup butter

¾ cup sugar

4 large eggs

1 cup all-purpose flour

½ teaspoon ground cinnamon

¼ teaspoon baking powder

¼ teaspoon ground red pepper

¼ teaspoon ground chipotle chile pepper

½ teaspoon kosher salt, divided

½ cup sliced almonds

2 teaspoons olive oil

1 teaspoon light brown sugar

Preheat the oven to 350 degrees. Butter a 9x13-inch baking dish.

Microwave the chocolate and butter in a large microwave-safe bowl on High for 1 to 1½ minutes or until melted, stirring at 30-second intervals. Whisk in the sugar. Add the eggs one at a time, whisking just until blended after each addition. Whisk in the flour, cinnamon, baking powder, red pepper, chile pepper and ¼ teaspoon salt until thoroughly mixed.

Pour the batter into the prepared baking dish. Stir together the almonds, olive oil, brown sugar and remaining salt. Sprinkle the almond mixture over the cake batter. Bake for 30 minutes. The center will be soft when the cake is done. Cool the cake on a wire rack for 5 minutes. Serve warm with your favorite vanilla ice cream.

All you need is love, but a little chocolate now and then doesn't hurt.
CHARLES M. SCHULZ

Molten Chocolate Cakes

4 squares Baker's semisweet baking chocolate

½ cup butter

1 cup powdered sugar

2 eggs

2 egg yolks (discard the egg whites)

6 tablespoons all-purpose flour

½ cup frozen whipped topping, thawed

Preheat the oven to 425 degrees. Butter four ¾-cup custard cups or soufflé dishes and place them on a baking sheet.

Microwave the chocolate and butter in a large microwave-safe bowl on High for 1 minute or until the butter is melted. Stir with a wire whisk until the chocolate is completely melted. Stir in the powdered sugar until well blended. Blend in the eggs and egg yolks with a wire whisk. Stir in the flour. Divide the batter between the prepared custard cups.

Bake for 13 to 14 minutes or until the sides are firm but the centers are soft. Let stand for 1 minute. Carefully run a small knife around the cakes to loosen. Invert the cakes onto dessert dishes. Serve immediately topped with the whipped topping.

NOTE: You can prepare the batter for this dessert a day ahead of time. Pour the batter into the prepared custard cups, cover with plastic wrap and refrigerate. Bake as directed when ready to serve.

If there ever comes a day where we can't be together, keep me in your heart; I'll stay there forever.

WINNIE THE POOH

Oatmeal Cake

CAKE

1¼ cups water

1 cup minute oats

½ cup butter, cut into small chunks

1 cup sugar

1 cup packed brown sugar

2 eggs, beaten

1⅓ cups all-purpose flour

1 teaspoon baking soda

½ teaspoon ground cinnamon

Pinch of salt

COCONUT PECAN ICING

½ cup butter

¼ cup evaporated milk

½ cup sugar

3½ ounces flaked coconut

1 cup chopped pecans

1 teaspoon vanilla extract

For the Cake, preheat the oven to 350 degrees. Grease and flour a 9x13-inch cake pan.

Boil the water in a saucepan. Combine the oats and butter in a bowl and pour the boiling water over the oats. Mix and let stand for 20 minutes or until the oats are softened and the water is absorbed.

Add the sugar, brown sugar and eggs to the oats mixture. Add the flour, baking soda, cinnamon and salt. Mix well using a spoon. Pour into the prepared cake pan and bake for 35 minutes. Let stand to cool slightly.

For the Coconut Pecan Icing, mix the butter, evaporated milk and sugar in a saucepan and bring to a boil. Add the coconut, pecans and vanilla and mix thoroughly.

Pour the Coconut Pecan Icing over the partially cooled cake. Broil in the oven for 5 to 7 minutes or until golden brown.

Springtime Blueberry Lemon Cake

This cake is so worth the time! It is a Fab Five favorite!

CAKE

Parchment paper

1½ cups cake flour

1½ cups all-purpose flour

2 teaspoons baking powder

¼ teaspoon baking soda

¾ teaspoon salt

2 cups sugar

1 cup unsalted butter, at room temperature

1 tablespoon lemon zest

4 large eggs

2 teaspoons lemon extract

½ teaspoon vanilla extract

¾ cup plus 2 tablespoons whole milk

¼ cup plus 2 tablespoons sour cream

2 tablespoons fresh lemon juice

2½ cups fresh blueberries, at room temperature, rinsed and drained well

LEMON CREAM CHEESE FROSTING

¾ cup unsalted butter, at room temperature

12 ounces cream cheese, softened

1 teaspoon vanilla extract

¼ teaspoon lemon extract

3 cups powdered sugar

Blueberries and lemon slices for garnish

For the Cake, preheat the oven to 350 degrees. Butter three 9-inch round cake pans and line the bottom of each with parchment paper. Butter the parchment paper and dust lightly with flour, shaking out any excess flour.

Sift the cake flour into a mixing bowl. Add the flour, baking powder, baking soda and salt and whisk for 30 seconds; set aside.

Whip the sugar, butter and lemon zest in a stand mixer using the paddle attachment until the mixture is pale and fluffy. Mix in the eggs one at a time. Stir in the lemon extract and vanilla extract.

Combine the milk, sour cream and lemon juice in a small bowl and mix well. Let stand for 3 minutes.

Toss the blueberries in a bowl with 3 tablespoons of the flour mixture.

Add a third of the remaining flour mixture alternately with half of the milk mixture to the sugar mixture, beginning and ending with the flour mixture and stirring just until mixed after each addition. Fold in the blueberries gently.

Divide the mixture evenly among the prepared cake pans. Bake for 24 to 27 minutes or until a wooden pick inserted into the center comes out clean. Cool completely.

For the Lemon Cream Cheese Frosting, whip the butter in a mixing bowl until the mixture is pale and fluffy. Add the cream cheese and mix until smooth and fluffy. Add the vanilla extract, lemon extract and powdered sugar. Blend for several minutes or until the mixture is smooth and fluffy. Chill the frosting for several minutes if slightly runny.

Frost the cake with the Lemon Cream Cheese Frosting and garnish with blueberries and lemon slices. Store in an airtight container.

Wanda's Strawberry Cake

This is Diane's mother's great cake. It is a family gathering must!

CAKE

- 1 package white cake mix
- 1 (3-ounce) package strawberry gelatin
- 4 eggs
- 2 (10-ounce) packages frozen strawberries, thawed (reserve ⅓ cup of the juice of the strawberries for the icing)
- 3 tablespoons all-purpose flour
- ¾ cup vegetable oil

STRAWBERRY ICING

- 6 tablespoons margarine
- ⅓ cup juice from the strawberries
- 16 ounces powdered sugar

For the Cake, preheat the oven to 350 degrees. Grease and flour a 9x13-inch cake pan.

Mix the cake mix, gelatin, eggs, strawberries, flour and oil in a bowl. Pour into the prepared cake pan.

Bake for 35 to 40 minutes or until a wooden pick inserted in the center comes out clean. Do not overcook. Let stand to cool completely.

For the Strawberry Icing, melt the margarine in a saucepan. Stir in the strawberry juice and powdered sugar. Ice the cake with the Strawberry Icing.

German Chocolate Cheesecake

CAKE
1 package German chocolate cake mix

CREAM CHEESE FILLING
2 (8-ounce) packages cream cheese, softened

1½ cups sugar

4 eggs, lightly beaten

GERMAN CHOCOLATE FROSTING
1 cup sugar

1 cup evaporated milk

½ cup butter, cubed (do not use margarine)

3 egg yolks, lightly beaten

1 teaspoon vanilla extract

2½ cups flaked coconut

1½ cups chopped pecans

For the Cake, preheat the oven to 325 degrees. Grease a 9x13-inch baking dish.

Prepare the cake batter according to the package directions; set aside (do not bake).

For the Cream Cheese Filling, beat the cream cheese and sugar in a small mixing bowl until smooth. Add the eggs and beat at low speed just until mixed.

Pour half of the cake batter into the prepared baking dish. Smooth with a spatula. Pour the cream cheese mixture carefully over the batter in the baking dish. Spoon the remaining batter carefully over the top; spread to the edge of the pan. Bake for 70 to 75 minutes or until a wooden pick inserted in the center comes out clean. Cool on a wire rack for 1 hour.

For the German Chocolate Frosting, combine the sugar, milk, butter and egg yolks in a heavy saucepan. Cook over medium-low heat until the mixture is thick enough to coat the back of a metal spoon or a thermometer reads 160 degrees, stirring constantly. Remove from the heat. Stir in the vanilla; fold in the coconut and pecans. Cool until the frosting reaches the desired consistency.

Frost the cooled cake. Refrigerate any leftover cake.

Creamy Pumpkin Squares

CRUST

1 package yellow cake mix

1 egg

½ cup butter, melted

FILLING

1 (8-ounce) package cream cheese, softened

2 eggs

1 teaspoon vanilla extract

½ cup butter, melted

1 (16-ounce) can pumpkin

1 teaspoon ground cinnamon

¼ teaspoon ground nutmeg

2 cups powdered sugar

Whipped topping or whipped cream and toasted pecans (optional)

For the Crust, preheat the oven to 350 degrees. Grease a 9x13-inch glass baking dish lightly.

Pour the dry cake mix into a bowl and break up any small lumps. Add the egg and butter; mix well. Press over the bottom of the prepared baking dish. Set aside.

For the Filling, beat the cream cheese in a mixing bowl until smooth. Add the eggs, vanilla and butter; beat until smooth. Mix in the pumpkin, cinnamon and nutmeg. Add the powdered sugar gradually, mixing well. Pour the filling over the crust and bake for 40 minutes. The center will be gooey when you take it out of the oven. Do not overbake. Let the squares cool completely. Top with a dollop of whipped topping and sprinkle with pecans.

Pumpkin Cheesecake with Toffee Sauce

Requires refrigeration overnight.

CHEESECAKE

1½ cups graham cracker crumbs

¾ cup crushed gingersnaps

½ cup pecan pieces

10 tablespoons butter, melted

Nonstick cooking spray

3½ (8-ounce) packages cream cheese, softened

1¼ cups brown sugar

5 eggs, at room temperature

1½ cups pumpkin purée

2 teaspoons vanilla extract

1 teaspoon ground cinnamon

½ teaspoon ground ginger

¼ teaspoon ground cloves

¼ teaspoon ground nutmeg

½ teaspoon salt

TOFFEE SAUCE

½ cup unsalted butter

1 cup light brown sugar

¾ cup heavy cream

½ cup chopped pecans

For the Cheesecake, preheat the oven to 350 degrees. Spray or grease a 9-inch springform pan.

Combine the graham cracker crumbs, gingersnaps and pecans in a large bowl and pour in the butter. Mix well until the mixture begins to look like wet sand. Spread half of the mixture over the bottom of the pan and pat the remaining half of the mixture on the sides of the pan. Bake for 8 to 10 minutes. Remove and let stand to cool.

Cream the cream cheese in a separate bowl until smooth. Blend in the brown sugar. Crack the eggs into a small bowl and add one at a time to the cream cheese mixture. Blend in the pumpkin purée and vanilla. Add the cinnamon, ginger, cloves, nutmeg and salt. Pour the mixture into the springform pan.

Seal by placing foil around the outside of the pan. Fill a large baking pan halfway with warm water and place the cheesecake inside the baking pan. Place both pans inside the oven and bake for 1 hour or until a wooden pick inserted in the middle comes out clean. Baking the cheesecake in warm water will keep the top from cracking.

Allow the cheesecake to cool at room temperature for 20 minutes. Remove the outside rim of the springform pan and place the cake in the refrigerator overnight.

For the Toffee Sauce, melt the butter in a large saucepan. Add the brown sugar and stir until thoroughly mixed. Pour in the cream and cook over medium-high heat for 5 minutes or until the toffee sauce is slightly boiling, stirring constantly; do not let it boil over. Stir in the pecans. Remove the sauce from the heat and allow to cool. Pour over the top of the cheesecake or serve on the side.

No one is born a great cook; one learns by doing.
JULIA CHILD

Pumpkin Cake Roll

There is nothing better in the Fall!

CAKE

3 eggs

1 cup sugar

⅔ cup canned pumpkin

1 teaspoon lemon juice

¾ cup all-purpose flour

1 teaspoon baking powder

2 teaspoons ground cinnamon

1 teaspoon ground ginger

½ teaspoon ground nutmeg

½ teaspoon salt

1 cup chopped pecans

Powdered sugar

FILLING

1 cup powdered sugar

2 (3-ounce) packages cream cheese, softened

4 tablespoons butter or margarine, at room temperature

½ teaspoon vanilla extract

For the Cake, preheat the oven to 375 degrees. Grease and flour a 10x15-inch jelly roll pan.

Beat the eggs at high speed in a mixing bowl for 5 minutes. Add the sugar gradually, beating constantly. Stir in the pumpkin and lemon juice. Stir together the flour, baking powder, cinnamon, ginger, nutmeg and salt in a separate bowl. Fold the flour mixture into the pumpkin mixture. Spread the batter in the prepared pan. Top with the pecans. Bake for 15 minutes.

Turn the cake out on a kitchen towel that has been sprinkled with powdered sugar. Roll the towel and the cake together, starting at the narrow end. Let stand to cool completely.

For the Filling, combine the powdered sugar, cream cheese, butter and vanilla in a mixing bowl and beat until smooth.

Unroll the cake and spread the filling over the top. Re-roll the cake and chill until serving time. Dust the roll with powdered sugar to serve.

Sally's Berrymisu

Sally Stuckey is a great Alabama cook.

- 1 (12-ounce) package frozen unsweetened raspberries, thawed
- 12 ounces cream cheese, softened
- 1½ cups plus 1 to 2 tablespoons sugar, divided
- 2 cups chilled whipping cream
- 1 cup water
- ½ cup fresh lemon juice
- 40 (about) ladyfingers (soft like sponge cake)
- Fresh raspberries for garnish
- Fresh mint sprigs for garnish

Purée the raspberries in a food processor until smooth. Strain into a medium bowl, pressing on the solids to extract as much liquid as possible and discarding the seeds in the strainer. Beat the cream cheese and ½ cup sugar in a large mixing bowl until smooth. Beat the whipping cream with 1 to 2 tablespoons sugar in another large bowl until peaks form. Fold the whipped cream gently into the cream cheese mixture. Fold in the puréed raspberries just until mixed.

Bring the remaining sugar, water and lemon juice to a boil in a small saucepan, stirring frequently. Cool slightly. Dip each ladyfinger briefly into the lemon syrup, turning to coat.

Arrange a layer of the ladyfingers, flat side up, in the bottom of a 12-cup trifle dish, trimming to fit if necessary. Spread a fourth of the raspberry mixture over the ladyfingers. Add a layer of biscuits. Repeat layering with more raspberry mixture, then biscuits; top with the remaining raspberry mixture.

Refrigerate, covered, for 3 to 24 hours to allow the flavors to marry. Garnish with raspberries and mint sprigs.

Sticky Toffee Pudding

STICKY TOFFEE SAUCE

3 cups heavy whipping cream, divided

1½ cups brown sugar

4 tablespoons butter

¼ cup light corn syrup

CAKE

¾ pound dates, pitted

1½ cups water

1½ cups all-purpose flour

1½ teaspoons baking powder

½ teaspoon baking soda

½ cup butter

¾ cup firmly packed brown sugar

3 large eggs

¼ cup heavy whipping cream

For the Sticky Toffee Sauce, boil 1½ cups of the whipping cream, brown sugar, butter and light corn syrup in a 6-quart pan over high heat for 6 to 8 minutes or until golden brown, stirring frequently. Remove from the heat and stir in the remaining whipping cream. Return to high heat and cook for 1 to 2 minutes or until the sauce comes to a rolling boil, stirring constantly. (Can cool and chill the sauce, covered, for up to 2 days and reheat, stirring frequently.)

For the Cake, preheat the oven to 325 degrees. Butter and flour a 9-inch square baking pan.

Combine the dates and water in a 4-quart saucepan. Boil over high heat for 5 to 7 minutes or until most of the liquid is absorbed, stirring frequently and watching carefully as the liquid reduces to avoid scorching. Let cool for at least 20 minutes.

Mix the flour with the baking powder and baking soda in a bowl. Process the cooked dates in a food processor until smooth. Add the butter, brown sugar, eggs and flour mixture; process until well blended. Spread the batter evenly in the prepared baking pan.

Bake for 30 to 40 minutes or until the cake springs back when lightly pressed in the center and the edges begin to pull from the sides of the pan. Let the cake cool in the pan for at least 5 minutes. Invert onto a wire rack. Let stand to cool. Cut the cake horizontally into halves.

Rinse and dry the baking pan. Pour about ½ cup hot Sticky Toffee Sauce into the pan. Return the bottom layer of the cake to the pan. Pour about 2 cups of the sauce evenly over the cake. Replace the top layer of the cake. Pour the remaining sauce evenly over the top. Let stand for at least 30 minutes or up to 1 hour. Cut into 9 equal squares. Pour the heavy cream over the top. Serve warm.

Peanut Butter Mousse Pie

From Debbie McBride, another dessert lover.

CRUST

1½ cups graham cracker crumbs
   or chocolate wafer crumbs

⅓ cup chopped peanuts

3 tablespoons sugar

⅓ cup unsalted butter, melted

FILLING

½ cup unsalted butter

¾ cup sugar

3 large eggs, separated

1 teaspoon vanilla extract

¾ pound smooth peanut butter, heated

2½ cups heavy cream, whipped

CHOCOLATE SAUCE

1 cup sugar

5 tablespoons cocoa, sifted

3 tablespoons all-purpose flour

1 cup milk

4 tablespoons unsalted butter

1 teaspoon vanilla extract

For the Crust, preheat the oven to 350 degrees. Grease a 10-inch springform pan.

Mix the graham cracker crumbs, peanuts, sugar and butter in a bowl. Press the graham cracker mixture into the prepared springform pan. Bake for 10 minutes. Set aside.

For the Filling, cream the butter in a mixing bowl until fluffy. Add the sugar, egg yolks and vanilla gradually, beating constantly. Fold in the peanut butter. Clean the metal bowl and beater well and wipe dry. Beat the egg whites in a separate bowl until stiff and fold into the peanut butter mixture. Fold in the whipped cream. Spoon the resulting mousse into the prepared springform pan and freeze.

For the Chocolate Sauce, combine the sugar, cocoa and flour in a saucepan. Stir until well blended. Stir in the milk and add the butter. Cook over low heat until thickened. Remove from the heat and stir in the vanilla. Pour into a storage container and allow to cool before refrigerating.

Remove the pie from the freezer 30 to 60 minutes before serving. Drizzle with Chocolate Sauce. Slice and serve.

NOTE: Try omitting the crust and serving the mousse in a pool of chocolate sauce, garnishing with chopped peanuts.

Chess Pie

Our dear friend Jonnie Delle Cogdell gave this recipe to us.

1 cup butter, at room temperature

1½ cups sugar

3 tablespoons all-purpose flour

4 eggs, lightly beaten

1½ cups half-and-half

½ teaspoon vanilla extract

½ teaspoon ground nutmeg

1 unbaked pie shell

Preheat the oven to 350 degrees.

Cream the butter and sugar in a mixing bowl. Beat in the flour. Add the eggs and mix well. Beat in the half-and-half, vanilla and nutmeg.

Pour the filling into the pie shell. Bake for 55 to 60 minutes or just until set. Let stand to cool completely to allow pie to set fully.

NOTE: Place a piece of foil on the oven rack below the rack the pie is baking on to catch splatters and drippings.

Our Favorite Lemon Bars

And who doesn't love a lemon bar!

1 cup butter, softened

2 cups all-purpose flour

½ cup sugar

4 eggs

1½ cups sugar

9 tablespoons fresh lemon juice

Powdered sugar

Preheat the oven to 350 degrees.

Combine the butter, flour and sugar in a mixing bowl and beat until crumbly. Press over the bottom of a 9x13-inch baking pan. Bake for 20 minutes or until the edges are browned. Whisk the eggs, sugar and lemon juice in a bowl until frothy. Pour over the hot crust. Bake for 18 to 20 minutes or just until set. Cool on a wire rack and dust with powdered sugar just before serving.

Pecan Squares

2 cups all-purpose flour

⅔ cup powdered sugar

¾ cup butter, at room temperature

½ cup firmly packed brown sugar

½ cup honey

⅔ cup butter

3 tablespoons whipping cream

3½ cups coarsely chopped pecans

Preheat the oven to 350 degrees. Grease a 9x13-inch baking dish lightly.

Sift the flour and the powdered sugar into a bowl. Cut in ¾ cup butter using a pastry blender or a fork just until the mixture resembles coarse meal.

Pat the mixture over the bottom and 1½ inches up the sides of the prepared baking dish. Bake for 20 minutes or until the edges are lightly browned. Let stand to cool.

Bring the brown sugar, honey, ⅔ cup butter and whipping cream to a boil in a saucepan over medium-high heat. Stir in the pecans. Pour the hot filling into the prepared crust.

Bake for 25 to 30 minutes or until golden brown and bubbly. Cool completely before cutting into 2-inch squares.

Salted Nut Bars

3 cups coarsely chopped salted peanuts (no skins), divided

2½ tablespoons butter

2 cups peanut butter chips

14 ounces sweetened condensed milk

2 cups miniature marshmallows

Kosher salt or sea salt (optional)

Place 1½ cups of the peanuts in the bottom of an ungreased 7x11-inch pan. Melt the butter and peanut butter chips in a large saucepan over low heat. Stir until smooth and remove from the heat. Stir in the condensed milk and the marshmallows. Continue stirring until smooth and well blended.

Pour the peanut butter mixture over the peanuts in the pan. Sprinkle the remaining peanuts over the top of the peanut butter mixture. Sprinkle lightly with salt. Cover and refrigerate until chilled. Cut into bars. Serve chilled or at room temperature.

NOTE: These can be made in a 9x13-inch pan if another cup of peanuts is divided between the bottom of the pan and the top of the bars. The same amount of filling will work and give you slightly thinner bars.

Susan Short's Awesome Apricot Bars

This is a secret family recipe, shared for the first time. Our sweet friend makes these when we beg her, and we all fight over the edges. You will love them! Perfect for any occasion.

Parchment paper
½ cup butter
1 package white cake mix
½ cup brown sugar

½ cup old-fashioned oats
1 cup flaked coconut
½ cup chopped pecans
1 cup apricot preserves

Preheat the oven to 350 degrees. Line a 9x13-inch baking dish with parchment paper that goes to the top edge of the dish on all sides.

Cut the butter into the cake mix and brown sugar with a pastry blender or 2 knives until the mixture is crumbly. Stir in the oats, coconut and pecans; set aside 1½ cups of the oats mixture. Press the remainder of the oats mixture over the bottom of the prepared baking dish. Stir the apricot preserves to soften and spread over the uncooked crust to within ½ inch of the edge. Sprinkle with the reserved oats mixture to cover. Bake for 30 to 35 minutes or until browned and bubbly.

Cool completely in the pan. Remove to a large cutting board by grasping the parchment paper and tipping the pan. Cut into small squares or cut into 24 squares and then cut each square diagonally to get 48 bite-size pieces.

NOTE: Recipe can be doubled and baked for 45 to 50 minutes in a 10x15-inch jelly roll pan.

Chocolate Toffee Cookies

Easy and good!

Nonstick cooking spray

1 package devil's food cake mix

⅓ cup vegetable oil

2 eggs

¾ cup coarsely chopped Heath or other chocolate-covered toffee bars

Preheat the oven to 350 degrees. Spray cookie sheets with nonstick cooking spray.

Combine the cake mix, vegetable oil and eggs in a large mixing bowl. Beat for 3 to 4 minutes or until well blended. Stir in the candy using a spoon. Drop by teaspoonfuls 2 inches apart onto prepared cookie sheets. Bake for 9 to 11 minutes or until firm. Remove the cookies to a wire rack to cool completely.

A balanced diet is a cookie in each hand.

BARBARA JOHNSON

Crunchy Praline Cookies

COOKIES

Parchment paper

2 cups all-purpose flour

¼ teaspoon salt

¼ teaspoon baking soda

½ cup unsalted butter, at room temperature

1 cup packed light brown sugar

1 large egg

1 tablespoon bourbon or freshly squeezed orange juice

FILLING

1 cup finely chopped pecans

½ cup packed dark brown sugar

½ teaspoon ground cinnamon

¼ cup sour cream

For the Cookies, preheat the oven to 350 degrees. Line 2 cookie sheets with parchment paper; set aside.

Sift the flour, salt and baking soda into a medium bowl. Cream the butter and brown sugar in a mixing bowl until light in color and well blended. Beat in the egg and bourbon. Add the flour mixture gradually and mix just until incorporated.

For the Filling, combine the pecans, dark brown sugar, cinnamon and sour cream in a small bowl and mix well. Set aside.

Shape the dough into 8 dozen ½-inch balls. Arrange the balls 1½ inches apart on the prepared cookie sheets. Insert the end of a wooden spoon into each ball and move the spoon around to make the largest hole possible. Fill each hole with ½ teaspoon of the filling. Bake for 8 to 10 minutes or until the filling melts into the cookies. Transfer the cookies to a wire rack to cool. Store in an airtight container for up to 1 week.

Pumpkin Orange Cookies

COOKIES

2½ cups all-purpose flour

½ teaspoon baking soda

½ teaspoon salt

1 cup butter, at room temperature

1 cup sugar

½ cup packed brown sugar

1 egg

1 (15-ounce) can pure pumpkin

2 tablespoons orange juice

1 teaspoon grated orange peel

½ cup chopped pecans or walnuts (optional)

ORANGE GLAZE

3 cups sifted powdered sugar

6 tablespoons orange juice

2 teaspoons grated orange peel

For the Cookies, preheat the oven to 375 degrees.

Combine the flour, baking soda and salt in a medium bowl. Combine the butter, sugar and brown sugar in a large mixing bowl and beat until creamy. Add the egg, pumpkin, orange juice and orange peel and beat until mixed. Add the flour mixture gradually, beating constantly. Beat just until the flour is incorporated. Stir in the pecans.

Drop the dough by rounded tablespoonfuls onto ungreased cookie sheets. Bake for 12 to 14 minutes or until the edges are set. Remove to wire racks to cool completely.

For the Orange Glaze, mix the powdered sugar, orange juice and orange peel in a medium bowl until smooth.

Spread each cookie with about ½ teaspoon of the Orange Glaze.

Lazy Day Spice Cookies

This recipe is from Phyllis' friend Jodi McDaniel

1 package spice cake mix

2 cups oats

2 eggs

½ cup packed brown sugar

1 teaspoon baking soda

1 teaspoon vanilla extract

1 cup vegetable oil

1 cup chopped pecans

1 cup raisins (optional)

Preheat the oven to 350 degrees.

Combine the cake mix, oats, eggs, brown sugar, baking soda, vanilla, vegetable oil, pecans and raisins in a bowl and mix well. Drop by spoonfuls onto ungreased cookie sheets. Bake for 10 to 12 minutes. Cool and store in an airtight container.

Easy Toffee

This recipe is from Debbie Earl. It is so good and an easy recipe to prepare. Great for holiday gift giving.

1 cup butter

1 cup sugar

6 chocolate candy bars

1 cup finely chopped pecans

Grease a cookie sheet with butter.

Cook the butter and sugar in a saucepan over medium-low to medium heat until caramel-colored, stirring constantly. Pour immediately onto the prepared cookie sheet. Place the candy on top of the toffee. Let stand just until the candy is melted. Smooth with a spatula. Sprinkle the nuts over the chocolate. Let cool completely and break into pieces.

Race for the Cure, Ft. Worth, Texas

FAB FIVE FAVORITES

We are pleased to include a chapter of favorite recipes from our first cookbook, *Always Enough Thyme For Great Friends, Fabulous Food, and Spirited Fun.* In the first book, we presented recipes in a menu format that replicated the many cooperative dinners we had prepared together. In this new cookbook, we offer our old favorites as individual recipes and hope you enjoy them as much as we have through all these years.

When we published *Always Enough Thyme*, we plunged into a marketing campaign with great enthusiasm. We started in Lubbock by setting up book-signing parties at the houses and businesses of our friends, and formal book signings at the local Barnes & Noble, Gourmet Pantry, and United Supermarket's Market Street. We received a long and laudatory article in the local newspaper, the *Lubbock Avalanche-Journal*, and generally became the talk of the town. The experience was absolutely invigorating. People loved the cookbook, and we loved making new friends, gathering with old friends, and talking food at every stop.

Soon, we realized the books were selling so well that we should get the word out all over Texas, so we organized book signings in our hometowns and any other place that would have us, including selling cookbooks in the Lubbock International Airport Gift Shop. As our market continued to grow, we were given some very exciting promotional opportunities. In Fort Worth, we were asked to be guest chefs at the Central Market Cooking School, where we cooked alongside the professionals, preparing a whole meal from recipes in our book and sharing every tasty morsel with an eager and engaged crowd of foodies. Naturally, our book was available for purchase, and we sold all we brought with us.

We also prepared an elaborate promotional gift basket for Bob Phillips, the host of *Texas Country Reporter*, a syndicated television program that features slice-of-life stories from around the Lone Star State. We filled the basket with everything Texas: margarita mix and glasses, salsa and tortilla chips, a replica cotton bale, and, of course, *Always Enough Thyme*. When we finally heard from him, he announced he would be in Lubbock in three days and would like to produce a feature on us. Fab Five members in Lubbock frantically called Debbie and Jan in Fort Worth to tell them to do everything they could to be in Lubbock for the shoot. Miraculously, they made it, and we were featured in three activities: lunching together, cooking together, and signing books together at Market Street. Our segment of *Texas Country Reporter* has aired innumerable times, and for being on the show, we were invited to participate in the *Texas Country Reporter* Festival, a jubilant annual happening held on the courthouse square in Waxahachie. We loved the event and sold a lot of books.

The highlight of our marketing efforts finally reached beyond Texas when *Southern Living* magazine decided to feature us in the November 2002 issue. The magazine flew a team to Lubbock that included the magazine editor, a stylist, a photographer, and a chef. From interior photos of our houses festooned for the holidays, they selected Phyllis' for the photo shoot, and we all gathered to be wined and dined on our own recipes by the delightful and accomplished *Southern Living* chef. After the session, we converged at Diane's house to prepare an elaborate spread for our new friends. It was a beautiful late autumn day, so we sat out on the patio, sharing food and stories, drinking more wine, and celebrating our love of cooking, eating, and good company. When the issue of *Southern Living* appeared on the stands, we bought up every copy we could get our hands on and gleefully distributed them to everyone we knew as a tribute to our cookbook and friendship.

Ultimately, we sold 15,000 copies of *Always Enough Thyme* through three printings, and the promotional adventure we had during the process stands as one of the peak experiences of our long and eventful relationship. Now, we are on the road again, celebrating the thrills of cooking and the delights of eating as we promote the recipes we've collected in our new book, and we all agree it's about time!

Always Enough Thyme Debut

Texas Country Reporter Filming

Southern Living Photo Shoot

Herbed Brunch Casserole

2½ cups herb-seasoned croutons

2 cups shredded sharp Cheddar cheese

4 ounces mushrooms, sliced

2 pounds bulk sausage

6 eggs

2½ cups milk

1 (10-ounce) can cream of mushroom soup

2¾ teaspoons dry mustard

Preheat the oven to 300 degrees. Grease a 9x13-inch baking dish.

Spread the croutons in a single layer in the prepared baking dish. Sprinkle the cheese and mushrooms evenly over the croutons. Cook the sausage in a large skillet for 15 minutes or until browned, stirring to crumble; drain. Spread evenly over the mushrooms. Beat the eggs, milk, soup and dry mustard in a medium bowl. Pour over the layers. Bake for 1½ hours or until set. Serve hot.

NOTE: The unbaked casserole can be refrigerated overnight.

Bubble Bread

⅓ cup Parmesan cheese

⅓ cup mayonnaise

1 loaf French bread

Preheat the oven to 400 degrees.

Combine the cheese and mayonnaise in a bowl and mix well. Cut the bread into 1-inch-thick slices. Spread the cheese mixture over the bread. Arrange on a baking sheet. Bake until hot and bubbly.

Pecan Casserole

Prepare the night before.

CASSEROLE

- 1 loaf cinnamon raisin bread, cubed
- 2 (12-count) packages sausage links, cubed
- 6 eggs
- 1½ cups milk
- 1½ cups half-and-half
- 1 teaspoon vanilla extract
- ¼ teaspoon ground nutmeg
- ¼ teaspoon ground cinnamon

TOPPING

- 1 cup packed brown sugar
- 1 cup coarsely chopped pecans
- ½ cup butter, softened
- 2 tablespoons maple syrup

For the Casserole, spread the bread in a greased 9x13-inch baking dish.

Brown the sausage in a large skillet; drain. Spread the sausage evenly over the bread. Combine the eggs, milk, half-and-half, vanilla, nutmeg and cinnamon in a medium bowl and mix well. Pour over the layers. Chill, covered, overnight.

Preheat the oven to 350 degrees.

For the Topping, mix the brown sugar, pecans, butter and maple syrup in a small bowl.

Sprinkle the topping over the casserole. Bake for 35 to 40 minutes.

Chicken Salad with Artichokes

The Fab Five's favorite salad. Great served over a bed of greens or on an onion roll as a sandwich.

4 chicken breast halves, cooked and cubed

1 (14-ounce) can artichoke hearts, drained and chopped

¾ cup mayonnaise

¾ cup chopped celery

6 green onions, chopped

1 cup chopped pecans, toasted

¼ teaspoon salt

⅛ teaspoon garlic powder

⅛ teaspoon pepper

Combine the chicken, artichokes, mayonnaise, celery, green onions, pecans, salt, garlic powder and pepper in a bowl and mix well. Chill, covered, until serving time.

NOTE: This can also be prepared in a food processor.

Granddad's Cornbread Salad

This is the best salad during tomato season.

1 recipe of cornbread (best made the night before)

2 green bell peppers, chopped

½ to 1 white onion, chopped

1 cup mayonnaise

1 tablespoon mustard

Salt and pepper to taste

3 large tomatoes, chopped

Crumble the cornbread into a large bowl. Stir in the bell peppers, onion, mayonnaise, mustard, salt and pepper. Add the tomatoes just before serving.

Watermelon and Avocado Salad

1 small red onion, very thinly
  sliced
2 tablespoons red wine vinegar
¼ (6-pound) watermelon
2 avocados
  Juice of 1 lime

Juice of 1 orange
2 teaspoons extra-virgin olive oil
1 cup loosely packed cilantro
  sprigs
  Salt and pepper to taste

Combine the onion and vinegar in a small bowl. Marinate, covered, in the refrigerator for several hours or overnight.

Cut the watermelon into 1½-inch chunks, discarding the rind and seeds. Cut the avocados into halves and remove the pits and peeling. Cut into 1-inch cubes and toss with the lime juice in a small bowl.

Toss the watermelon, avocado, orange juice, olive oil and cilantro in a large bowl, reserving some cilantro sprigs for garnish. Drain the onion and add to the salad. Sprinkle with salt and pepper. Toss again and garnish with the reserved cilantro.

Avocado Roasted Corn Guacamole

1 cup fresh corn kernels, or frozen corn kernels, thawed

3 tablespoons corn oil, divided

2 large avocados, cut into ½-inch cubes

1 large tomato, cut into ¼-inch cubes

¼ cup chopped fresh cilantro

2 tablespoons minced red onion

1 teaspoon (about) minced fresh or pickled jalapeño

1 teaspoon minced garlic

2 tablespoons fresh lime juice

1 teaspoon cider vinegar

1½ teaspoons coarse kosher salt

¼ teaspoon ground cumin

Preheat the oven to 450 degrees. Combine the corn and 1 tablespoon of the corn oil in a bowl and toss to coat. Spread on a baking sheet. Roast for 7 to 8 minutes or until golden brown, tossing frequently. Let stand to cool. Transfer to a medium bowl.

Fold in the avocados, tomato, cilantro, onion, jalapeño and garlic. Stir in the lime juice, vinegar, salt, cumin and the remaining corn oil. Chill, covered, for up to 6 hours. Serve with tortilla chips.

Fiesta Dip

Always the "hit" at a party.

2 pounds Monterey Jack cheese, shredded

1 (4-ounce) can olives, sliced

1 (4-ounce) can green chilies, chopped

1 bunch of green onions, chopped

4 tomatoes, chopped

1 (8-ounce) bottle Italian salad dressing

¼ cup chopped fresh parsley

¼ cup chopped fresh cilantro

Combine the cheese, olives, chilies, green onions, tomatoes, salad dressing, parsley and cilantro in a bowl and mix well. Serve with Fritos Scoops.

Marinated Shrimp

This recipe is so good it will have your guests coming back for more!

- 2 pounds (41 count or larger) shrimp, peeled and deveined with tails intact
- 2 medium white or purple onions, or a mixture, sliced into rings
- 1 cup vegetable oil

- 1½ cups white vinegar
- ½ cup sugar
- 1½ teaspoons salt
- 1½ teaspoons celery seed
- 4 tablespoons capers with juice

Place the shrimp in enough boiling salted water to cover. Reduce the heat and simmer for 3 to 5 minutes or until the shrimp are pink and tender. Drain the shrimp and rinse with cold water. Place in a large bowl and chill.

Alternate layers of the shrimp and onions in a sealable container. Mix the oil, vinegar, sugar, salt, celery seed and capers in a bowl and pour over the shrimp and onions. Seal and chill for at least 6 hours, shaking and/or inverting several times. Drain and serve.

NOTE: When deveining shrimp, make a partial cut through the shrimp. This will allow the flavors to penetrate the shrimp better. Also, if possible, prepare the shrimp the night before you want to serve them. They will be more flavorful if marinated a full day.

Shrimp and Wild Rice Casserole

Fabulous casserole! Expensive to make but absolutely worth every dime.

- 4 green onions including green tops, chopped
- 1 garlic clove, minced
- 1 small green bell pepper, chopped
- 4 tablespoons butter
- 2 pounds shrimp, cooked and deveined
- 2 packages long grain and wild rice, cooked
- 2 (10-ounce) cans cream of chicken soup
- 1 cup mayonnaise
- 1 (2-ounce) jar pimentos
- 1 (16-ounce) can green beans, well drained
- 1 (5-ounce) can sliced water chestnuts, drained
- 1 cup grated Monterey Jack cheese
- 1 cup grated Cheddar cheese
- ½ cup grated Parmesan cheese
- Dash of Tabasco sauce
- Dash of Worcestershire sauce
- Salt and pepper to taste
- 1 cup buttered breadcrumbs

Preheat the oven to 350 degrees. Grease a 9x13-inch baking dish.

Sauté the green onions, garlic and bell pepper in the butter in a large saucepan until tender. Add the shrimp, rice, soup, mayonnaise, pimentos, green beans, water chestnuts, Monterey Jack cheese, Cheddar cheese, Parmesan cheese, Tabasco sauce, Worcestershire sauce, salt and pepper; mix until blended. Pour into the prepared baking dish. Sprinkle with the breadcrumbs and bake for 30 minutes. This casserole freezes well.

Gourmet Chicken Casserole

This is a Fab Five favorite. It will be yours, too.

2 cups diced cooked chicken

¼ cup mayonnaise

1 cup cooked rice

½ teaspoon salt

1 (4-ounce) can sliced
mushrooms

1 cup diced celery

1 tablespoon lemon juice

1 tablespoon chopped onion

½ cup sliced almonds

1 (10-ounce) can cream of
chicken soup

1 cup crushed cornflakes

2 tablespoons butter, melted

Preheat the oven to 350 degrees. Butter a 9x13-inch casserole dish.

Combine the chicken, mayonnaise, rice, salt, mushrooms, celery, lemon juice, onion, almonds and soup in a bowl and mix well. Spoon into the prepared casserole dish. Mix the cornflakes and butter in a bowl and spread over the chicken mixture. Bake for 30 to 40 minutes.

Green Bean Bundles

Our husbands love this vegetable.

5 or 6 slices of bacon

3 or 4 (14-ounce) cans whole
green beans, or 1 pound fresh
green beans, cooked

½ cup packed brown sugar

4 tablespoons butter, melted

1 tablespoon Dijon mustard

Preheat the oven to 350 degrees. Cut the bacon into halves. Wrap each piece of bacon around 8 to 10 green beans. Secure each bundle using a wooden pick and place in a glass baking dish.

Combine the brown sugar, butter and mustard in a bowl and mix well. Spoon a portion of the mixture onto each bundle. Bake for 25 to 30 minutes or until the bacon is cooked through.

Green Chile Chicken or Beef Enchiladas

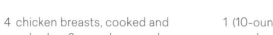

4 chicken breasts, cooked and cubed, or 2 pounds ground beef, browned and drained

1 small onion, chopped

2 to 3 teaspoons garlic powder

Salt and pepper to taste

1 pound shredded Velveeta cheese

1 can evaporated milk

1 (10-ounce) can cream of chicken soup

1 (10-ounce) can cream of mushroom soup

1 (4-ounce) can chopped green chilies

25 tortillas

½ cup vegetable oil

1 to 1½ cups grated Monterey Jack cheese

Preheat the oven to 350 degrees.

Combine the chicken, onion, garlic powder, salt and pepper in a bowl and mix well. Combine the Velveeta cheese, evaporated milk, cream of chicken soup, cream of mushroom soup and green chilies in a large saucepan; cook until the cheese is melted, stirring frequently.

Soften the tortillas by heating them in the vegetable oil in a skillet. Remove to paper towels to drain. Place a tortilla on a work surface and add a spoonful of the chicken mixture and a small amount of Monterey Jack cheese to each tortilla. Roll up the tortillas as tightly as possible and place in a casserole dish. Repeat this procedure with each tortilla. Pour the Velveeta cheese mixture over the enchiladas. Bake until hot and bubbly.

Praline Sweet Potatoes

SWEET POTATOES

3 cups cooked and mashed
sweet potatoes

1 cup sugar

2 eggs

1 teaspoon vanilla extract

⅓ cup milk

½ cup butter or margarine

1 cup brown sugar

TOPPING

⅓ cup all-purpose flour

⅓ cup butter

1 cup chopped pecans

Preheat the oven to 350 degrees.

For the Sweet Potatoes, combine the sweet potatoes, sugar, eggs, vanilla, milk, butter and brown sugar in a large mixing bowl and beat until smooth. Spoon into a 9x13-inch baking dish.

For the Topping, combine the flour, butter and pecans in a small bowl and stir until crumbly.

Sprinkle the topping over the sweet potatoes just before baking. Bake for 30 minutes. Can be made ahead and frozen.

Pecan Pie Cake

Absolutely divine! Serve warm, and they won't stop raving.

3 cups finely chopped pecans, toasted, divided

½ cup butter or margarine, softened

½ cup shortening

2 cups sugar

5 large eggs, separated

1 tablespoon vanilla extract

2 cups all-purpose flour

1 teaspoon baking soda

1 cup buttermilk

¾ cup dark corn syrup

Pecan Pie Filling (recipe follows)

Pastry Garnishes (recipe follows)

Preheat the oven to 350 degrees. Sprinkle 2 cups of the pecans evenly into 3 generously buttered 9-inch round cake pans; shake to coat bottoms and sides of the pans.

Combine the butter and shortening in a large mixing bowl and beat at medium speed with an electric mixer until fluffy. Add the sugar gradually, beating well. Add the egg yolks one at a time, beating until blended after each addition. Stir in the vanilla.

Combine the flour and baking soda in a small bowl and mix well. Add the flour mixture to the sugar mixture, alternately with the buttermilk, beginning and ending with the flour mixture and beating at low speed until blended after each addition. Stir in the remaining pecans.

Beat the egg whites at medium speed in a medium mixing bowl until stiff peaks form; fold a third of the egg whites into the batter. Fold in the remaining egg whites; do not overmix. Pour the batter into the prepared pans.

Bake for 25 minutes or until the layers test done. Cool in the pans on wire racks for 10 minutes. Invert the layers onto waxed paper-lined wire racks. Brush the tops and sides of the layers with the corn syrup. Cool completely.

Place the first cake layer, pecan side up, on a cake plate. Spread half of the Pecan Pie Filling over the layer. Add the second layer, pecan side up; spread with the remaining filling. Top with the remaining layer, pecan side up.

Arrange the Pastry Garnishes on and around the cake.

Pecan Pie Filling

½ cup firmly packed dark brown sugar

¾ cup dark corn syrup

⅓ cup cornstarch

4 egg yolks

1½ cups half-and-half

⅛ teaspoon salt

3 tablespoons butter or margarine

1 teaspoon vanilla extract

Whisk the brown sugar, corn syrup, cornstarch, egg yolks, half-and-half and salt in a heavy 3-quart saucepan until smooth. Bring the mixture to a boil over medium heat, whisking constantly. Boil for 1 minute or until thickened. Remove from the heat and whisk in the butter and vanilla.

Pour the filling into a medium bowl and place a sheet of waxed paper directly on the surface of the mixture to prevent a film from forming. Chill the mixture for 4 hours.

NOTE: To chill filling quickly, pour filling into a bowl. Place the bowl in a larger bowl filled with ice. Whisk constantly for 15 minutes or until cool.

Pastry Garnishes
for Pecan Pie Cake

1 (14-ounce) package
  refrigerated piecrusts

1 large egg

1 tablespoon water

Nonstick cooking spray

24 pecan halves

Preheat the oven to 425 degrees. Grease a baking sheet lightly.

Unfold the piecrusts and place on waxed paper. Press out the fold lines in the piecrusts. Cut 8 to 10 leaves from each piecrust using a 3-inch leaf-shape cutter and mark leaf veins using the tip of a knife. Reserve the pastry trimmings. Whisk the egg and water in a small bowl. Brush the egg mixture over the pastry leaves.

Crumple 10 to 12 small pieces of aluminum foil into ½-inch balls. Coat the foil pieces with nonstick cooking spray and place on the prepared baking sheet. Drape a pastry leaf over each ball (this gives the leaves movement and variety). Place the remaining pastry leaves on the baking sheet.

Bake for 6 to 8 minutes or until golden brown. Cool on a wire rack for 10 minutes. Remove the foil carefully from the leaves.

Preheat the oven to 350 degrees. Grease a baking sheet lightly. Pinch 12 pea-size pieces from the pastry trimmings. Place a piece of the pastry between 2 pecan halves, forming a sandwich. Repeat with the remaining pastry pieces and pecan halves. Cut the remaining pastry into 2-inch pieces; wrap the pastry pieces around one end of each pecan sandwich, leaving jagged edges to resemble half-shelled pecans. Brush with the egg mixture. Arrange on the prepared baking sheet. Bake for 10 minutes or until golden brown. Cool on a wire rack.

French Bread Pudding with Whiskey Sauce

You and your company will love this bread pudding.

BREAD PUDDING

1 cup sugar

½ cup butter, softened

5 eggs, beaten

1 pint heavy cream

Dash of ground cinnamon

1 tablespoon vanilla extract

¼ cup raisins (optional)

12 (1-inch-thick) slices of fresh or stale bread, crusts removed

WHISKEY SAUCE

1 cup sugar

1 cup heavy cream

Dash of ground cinnamon

1 tablespoon unsalted butter

½ teaspoon cornstarch

¼ cup water

1 tablespoon bourbon

For the Bread Pudding, preheat the oven to 350 degrees.

Cream the sugar and butter in a large mixing bowl. Add the eggs, cream, cinnamon, vanilla and raisins and mix well. Pour into a 9-inch square baking pan.

Arrange the bread in the egg mixture and let stand for 5 minutes to soak up some of the liquid. Turn the bread over and let stand for 10 minutes longer. Push the bread down so that most of it is covered by the egg mixture. Do not tear the bread.

Place the pan in a larger pan filled with water to ½ inch from the top. Cover with aluminum foil. Bake for 35 to 40 minutes. Uncover and bake for 10 minutes longer or until brown but still soft.

For the Whiskey Sauce, combine the sugar, cream, cinnamon and butter in a saucepan. Bring to a boil. Mix the cornstarch and water in a small bowl and add to the sauce. Cook until the sauce is transparent, stirring constantly. Remove from the heat and stir in the bourbon.

Serve the bread pudding immediately with the Whiskey Sauce.

Pumpkin Cheesecake Bars

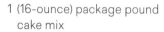

1 (16-ounce) package pound cake mix

3 eggs, divided

2 tablespoons butter, melted

4 teaspoons pumpkin pie spice, divided

8 ounces cream cheese, softened

½ teaspoon salt

1 (14-ounce) can sweetened condensed milk

1 (16-ounce) can pumpkin

1 cup chopped nuts

Preheat the oven to 350 degrees. Beat the cake mix, 1 egg, butter and 2 teaspoons pumpkin pie spice on low speed in a large mixing bowl until crumbly. Press over the bottom of a 9x13-inch baking pan. Set aside.

Beat the cream cheese in a large mixing bowl until fluffy. Add the remaining pumpkin pie spice, remaining eggs and salt gradually, beating constantly. Mix in the condensed milk and pumpkin. Pour over the crust. Sprinkle with the nuts. Bake for 30 to 40 minutes or until set. Let stand to cool. Chill in the refrigerator. Cut into bars to serve. Store leftovers in the refrigerator.

Tartly Frosted Lemon Squares

SQUARES

1 (3-ounce) can flaked coconut

2 eggs, separated

1 (14-ounce) can sweetened condensed milk

⅓ cup fresh lemon juice

4 tablespoons butter, melted

¼ cup all-purpose flour

½ teaspoon salt

LEMON FROSTING

1 cup powdered sugar

2 tablespoons butter, melted

1 tablespoon fresh lemon juice

For the Squares, preheat the oven to 350 degrees. Spread the coconut over the bottom of a 9x9-inch baking dish.

Beat the egg yolks in a large mixing bowl. Add the condensed milk, lemon juice and butter and beat until smooth. Stir in the flour and salt. Beat the egg whites in a small mixing bowl until stiff peaks form. Fold the egg whites into the batter. Pour into the prepared baking dish. Bake for 25 to 30 minutes.

For the Lemon Frosting, combine the powdered sugar, butter and lemon juice in a small bowl and stir until smooth.

Cut the baked layer into squares. Spread the Lemon Frosting over the squares.

Potato Chip Cookies

Sounds a little strange, but you will love them. This is one of our all-time favorite recipes.

- 1 cup butter, softened
- ½ cup sugar
- 1 teaspoon vanilla extract
- 1½ cups sifted all-purpose flour
- ¾ cup crushed potato chips
- ½ cup chopped pecans
- Sifted powdered sugar

Preheat the oven to 325 degrees.

Cream the butter and sugar in a mixing bowl. Stir in the vanilla, flour, potato chips and pecans. Drop onto ungreased cookie sheets. Bake for 15 to 18 minutes. Sprinkle with powdered sugar using a sifter. These cookies are very fragile.

NOTE: Use only salted, smooth potato chips—no barbecue, Ruffles, Pringles or similar.

Garlic and Rosemary Beef Tenderloin

The best marinade we have ever had!

- ½ cup olive oil
- ½ cup soy sauce
- ¼ cup balsamic vinegar or red wine vinegar
- 8 large garlic cloves, minced
- 4 teaspoons dried rosemary crumbled
- 1 (4- to 6-pound) beef tenderloin, trimmed
- Pepper to taste

Combine the olive oil, soy sauce, vinegar, garlic and rosemary in a glass baking dish. Add the tenderloin and turn to coat. Season generously with pepper. Cover and refrigerate the steak overnight, turning occasionally.

Remove the steak from the marinade and bring to room temperature. Grill over hot coals or bake in the oven at 350 degrees to an internal temperature of 125 degrees for rare or to an internal temperature of 150 degrees for medium.

Seasoned Peppers and Onions

⅓ cup olive oil

2 large onions, cut into 1-inch pieces

2 large red bell peppers, cut into 1-inch pieces

1 green bell pepper, cut into 1-inch pieces

¾ teaspoon dried marjoram, crumbled

⅛ teaspoon crushed red pepper

Salt and pepper to taste

Heat the olive oil in a large heavy skillet over medium-high heat. Add the onions, red bell peppers and green bell pepper. Sauté for 8 minutes or until the vegetables are beginning to soften. Add the marjoram and crushed red pepper. Season with salt and pepper. Cook for 2 minutes, stirring frequently.

Southern Hash Brown Casserole

1 (2-pound) package frozen hash brown potatoes, thawed

½ cup butter or margarine, melted

½ teaspoon black pepper

2 teaspoons salt

¼ teaspoon ground cumin

½ cup chopped onion

1 (10-ounce) can cream of chicken soup

1 cup sour cream

1 cup half-and-half

10 ounces Cheddar cheese, grated

Preheat the oven to 325 degrees. Mix the potatoes, butter, pepper, salt, cumin, onion, soup, sour cream, half-and-half and cheese in a large bowl. Pour into a 9x13-inch baking dish and bake for 1½ to 2 hours.

Footnotes

Non-Alcoholic Substitutions

White wine: Substitute with white grape juice; ginger ale; chicken or vegetable broth

Red wine: Substitute with grape juice; cranberry juice; chicken, beef, or vegetable broth; flavored vinegar; tomato juice

Brandy: Substitute with white grape juice; apple juice; cherry, peach, or apricot syrup

Beer: Substitute with chicken, beef, or mushroom broth; white grape juice; ginger ale

Rum: Substitute with pineapple juice combined with almond extract or molasses; vanilla extract

Sherry: Substitute with vanilla extract; orange or pineapple juice

Chocolate

Chocolate is very sensitive to sudden changes in temperature, so be sure to store it in a cool, dry place and avoid humidity.

Don't discard chocolate if it becomes gray. This film is not harmful, and the chocolate will return to normal once melted.

Citrus Tricks

Although there are different kinds of lemons, in most cases they aren't sold under different names. Generally, smaller lemons with smoother skin tend to have more juice.

To get the most juice out of fresh lemons, bring them to room temperature and roll them under your palm against the kitchen counter before squeezing, or microwave them on High for 30 seconds before squeezing.

Hamburger Tips

Mix the meat with the desired spices. Make patties. Refrigerate for a minimum of 2 hours. Go straight from refrigerator to grill. Patties won't stick! Press thumb in center of patty—keeps the patty from rounding up (puffing) and cooks patty evenly.

Miscellaneous Tips

Rub lean meats, such as pork tenderloin, flank steak, or chicken, with spice rubs, or marinate them; freeze in resealable plastic freezer bags. When thawed, meats will be perfectly seasoned and ready to go on the grill.

A good knife is a sharp knife. A chef's knife is ideal for most chopping needs. Use a paring knife for coring and peeling fruits and veggies.

Flatten thick, boneless chicken pieces with a meat mallet for more even cooking. Cover with plastic wrap before pounding, and do not over pound. When you pound them, the flesh becomes more porous, so it absorbs additional seasonings from rubs and marinades.

Use a zester to remove the fragrant rinds from oranges, lemons, and limes to add flavor to dishes with virtually no calories.

To prepare fresh breadcrumbs, cut the crusts off three thick slices of French bread. Tear the bread into large pieces and grind into fine crumbs in a food processor.

A flat whisk is perfect for stirring cooktop sauces because it reaches into all the corners.

flavor optimization, take cheese out of the refrigerator for n hour prior to serving.

make a garnish of Parmesan shavings.

king. The salt will draw the liquid

Add a dash of nutmeg to a white sauce for a great taste.

How do restaurants serve such tender, moist chicken? They submerge the breast in buttermilk for 3 to 4 hours under refrigeration.

To prevent condensation from forming an unappealing icy crust on ice cream, you can press waxed paper against its surface before you close the container. Follow this process each time, and every scoop will taste as fresh as the first.

Many recipes call for freshly grated gingerroot, which can be a challenge because the fibers separate messily from the root's juicy flesh. However, if you store the whole unpeeled root in the freezer, it will grate cleanly. Wrapped tightly in plastic wrap, unpeeled ginger will keep frozen for several months. When you wish to grate some, simply peel the part you need while it's still frozen, and return the remainder to the freezer.

Stuff a miniature marshmallow in the bottom of a sugar cone to prevent ice cream drips.

Use a meat baster to "squeeze" your pancake batter onto the hot griddle—perfectly shaped pancakes every time.

To prevent eggshells from cracking, add a dash of vinegar to the water before hard-boiling.

Run your hands under cold water before pressing Rice Krispies treats in the pan; the marshmallows won't stick to your fingers.

To easily remove burnt-on food from your skillet, simply add a drop or two of dish soap to enough water to cover the bottom of the pan, and bring to a boil on the stove.

Spray your plastic storage containers with nonstick cooking spray before pouring in tomato-based sauces—no more stains.

When a cake recipe calls for flouring the baking pan, use a bit of the dry cake mix instead. No white mess on the outside of the cake.

If you accidentally oversalt a dish while it's still cooking, drop in a peeled potato; it will absorb the excess salt.

Wrap celery in aluminum foil when putting in the refrigerator—it will keep for weeks.

Brush a beaten egg white over piecrust before baking to yield a beautiful glossy finish.

When boiling corn on the cob, add a pinch of sugar to help bring out the corn's natural sweetness

To determine whether an egg is fresh, immerse it in a pan of cool, salted water. If it sinks, it is fresh; if it rises to the surface, throw it away.

Don't throw out all that leftover wine (what leftover wine??). Freeze into ice cubes for future use in casseroles and sauces.

Resist the urge to flatten burgers with a spatula during grilling. The burgers will lose precious juices and will not cook any faster.

Before lighting the grill, spray the grill rack generously with non-stick cooking spray (never while warm or hot) to help keep fish from sticking.

To chop canned tomatoes, snip them with kitchen shears while still in the can. For fresh herbs, put in a measuring cup and snip the same way.

Use a melon baller to seed tomatoes.

The secret to keeping the crust of a fruit pie from getting soggy is egg white. The proteins bond together and form a wall that prevents the filling's juices from seeping into the crust. Lightly beat an egg white; then brush it over the inside of the uncooked shell before adding the fruit mixture. The coating will set as the pie bakes and keep your dessert crisp.

If you love green chilies like we do, try roasting Hatch green chiles in the late summer and separating and freezing in small batches. Then you can enjoy them all year in your soups, pastas, and casseroles.

Storing Vegetables

When storing veggies in plastic bags, make sure to poke some holes in the bag to allow for proper air circulation. Or buy perforated plastic vegetable bags.

Keep vegetables and fruits in separate produce drawers because some fruits, such as apples and pears, produce a substance called ethylene that hastens ripening of other produce.

Add crispness back to limp veggies like celery and asparagus by placing them stem side down in a small amount of water; refrigerate until crisp.

Do not wash vegetables until you're ready to eat them.

Fab Five Kids Get Married!

Amanda and Connor

Kristin and Bryan

The Fab Five Through
the Years

IN MEMORY OF MACKY MCKEE

DECEMBER 21, 1938–OCTOBER 17, 2010

Life is not measured by the breaths you take,
but by the moments that take your breath away.

UNKNOWN

Renee Stegar Simpson

About the Artist

Renee Steger Simpson

We are proud to feature the cover art of Lubbock artist Renee Steger Simpson and join Simpson's ever growing watercolor series entitled *Snooty Women*®. The *Snooty Women* series grew out of a combination of professional relationships that began to germinate in her art in October of 1992, beginning with a few intuitive marks that quickly evolved into a form revealing her ironic feelings about particular people and situations. As of the year 2015, Simpson has created over 300 watercolors in the series, with most now on display in private as well as corporate collections.

Today, Simpson divides her time between her private accounting practice and her art, often traveling to New Mexico to paint and teach. She is represented in Taos, New Mexico, by Bryan's Gallery and exhibits in galleries throughout the United States and abroad.

Artist Statement

I was raised with an artistic influence from my grandfather, who was a prolific painter. From early childhood, I was permitted to play in his studio. I also spent a great deal of time watching and absorbing, which has been a continuous source of inspiration in my life as well as my work. With my expression of life through color and shape, I hope to release emotion and add a quality to the spirited side of life that often escapes us! I work primarily in watercolor because the unpredictability and challenge of the medium coincides with all of my expectations of creativity.

Index

9